Estate Planning for IRAs and 401Ks

A Handbook for Individuals, Advisors and Attorneys

Explanation and Sample Forms

James G. Blase, CPA, JD, LLM

Table of Contents

Attorneys, CPAs, advisors and other individuals should not rely on this book or the forms contained herein, and should conduct their own independent examination of applicable law. Mr. Blase is not responsible for any loss caused by relying on the validity of the contents of any portion of this book.

I

Navigating The New Estate Planning Realities

Commentators appear to be almost uniform in proclaiming the demise of so-called stretch IRAs and 401Ks after the SECURE Act was signed in late December of 2020. Before 2020, designated beneficiaries could stretch the receipt of IRA and 401K plan (and other defined contribution plan) benefits over their entire lifetimes. The new rule, however, provides that the benefits must be paid out within 10 years of the account owner's death - years when the designated beneficiaries are likely to be in their highest income tax brackets.

For example, with certain exceptions (including those for a surviving spouses) a designated beneficiary having a 30-year life expectancy who previously could have delayed receiving IRA or plan benefits over 30 years must now fully withdraw the benefits within 10 years of the plan participant's or IRA owner's death. There is no set schedule for distributing the funds during those 10 years, as long as they are all withdrawn by the end.

The Nature of the Problem

Under the new law, not only must all of the tax on IRAs and plans benefits be paid much earlier than before, but the tax rate will likely be much higher too, since that income will be bundled into recipients' peak earning years.

Let's take an example of how the new law changes things. Let's say we have an IRA owner who dies and leaves a $1 million IRA. The designated beneficiary is 60 years old and expected to live another 25 years. We assume the IRA's income/growth rate is 5%. We're also assuming there's a 20% combined income tax rate on the income generated by withdrawn funds invested outside of the IRA.

Under the old law, if the beneficiary took only the required minimum distributions over his or her 25-year life expectancy, the after-tax value of the IRA distributions when the designated beneficiary was age 85 would be $2,204,122. (We're assuming there's a 30% combined federal and state tax rate since most of the income would not be in the beneficiary's peak earning years.)

Now let's look at what happens under the new law. If we assume that the beneficiary will take equal payments over 10 years, the after-tax payments would be $82,731 (based on a standard amortization table at 5% and a 35% combined federal and state income tax rate). Once removed from the taxable accounts, after 25 years the payments would grow to $1,854,391, after-tax, again assuming a 20% combined income tax rate on the reinvested funds.

Now let's assume the designated beneficiary waits until the end of year 10 to take the entire IRA balance. Here we assume there's a 40% combined federal and state tax rate on the lump sum, since the beneficiary will be in an even higher income tax bracket. The after-tax amount after 25 years would be $1,760,242, or approximately 5% less than the strategy of spreading the IRA distributions equally over 10 years, again assuming a 20% combined income tax rate on the reinvested funds. The $2,204,122 result under the old law is about 19% more than the best scenario under the new law, since it spreads out payments even further and at an even lower income tax rate.

Planning Alternatives

There are a number of alternatives an individual can consider in order to dampen the new law's tax effects. The major alternatives will be briefly explored and tested here:

1. Immediately begin converting to Roth IRAs. The basic theory here is to immediately begin withdrawing *significant* additional penalty-free amounts from IRAs, etc.,[1] even during the account holder's working years, with the anticipation that the withdrawn amounts will be taxed at a lower income rate than they would be later (e.g., after the sunset of the current low income tax rates in 2026), and then reinvest the withdrawn amounts in a Roth IRA.

Does this plan make sense? Let's assume the combined federal and state income tax rate for the IRA owner or designated beneficiary on early withdrawals (by the account owner) and withdrawals under the new 10-year withdrawal rule (by the designated beneficiary) is 35%, but that there's only a 20% combined federal and state tax rate on the investments purchased with the after-tax withdrawals.

---

[1]Including, potentially, substantially equal periodic payments pursuant to IRC Section 72(t).

(Remember, the tax rate on capital gains could be as little as 0% if beneficiaries hold the investments until they die.) The numbers can be run a variety of different ways, but in most situations it won't make sense mathematically to pay income taxes early—at least at *significantly higher* tax rates than the individual would have paid by maximizing the income tax deferral available during the individual's lifetime.

In some scenarios, the strategy can actually reduce the after-tax amount ultimately available to the individuals and their family. The individuals are accelerating the income tax payable during their lifetimes, at a significantly higher income tax rate, and not taking advantage of the new law's full 10-year income tax deferral after they die. If the account owner has not retired, the negatives associated with accelerating taxable IRA withdrawals are self-evident.

Before doing any significant Roth conversion during an individual's working years, in order to minimize income taxes to the designated beneficiaries, the individual must be mindful of the various potential negative aspects of the Roth conversion:

a. There is likely going to be a significantly higher income tax rate payable by the owner under a Roth conversion than there would be by taking minimum required distributions during the owner's lifetime. There is also the time value of the taxes saved by not converting.

b. The taxable growth in the after-tax required minimum distributions ("RMDs") can be controlled, and in any event the growth will receive a stepped-up income tax basis at the death of the account owner. This eliminates all income taxes on this growth in the after-tax distributions up until the time of the account owner's death.

c. Only 10 years of tax-free Roth deferral after the account owner's death are permitted under the new law. This undermines the post-death tax benefits available to Roth IRAs under the old law.

d. The IRA owner may need to use the IRA funds themselves to pay the conversion tax, and therefore be converting much less than the entirety of the IRA distribution.

An Optional Approach. One early withdrawal option (which is explored more fully in chapters II and III) that may produce significant income tax saving benefits, however, would be to wait until retirement, and then apply an amortization approach to the withdrawals. Under this **retirement amortization plan ("RAP")**, *beginning when the account owner is retired,* the owner can determine his or her (or joint, if married) approximate life expectancy, and then take withdrawals over this period plus 10 years (i.e., the beneficiaries' required withdrawal period).

For example, if a married couple are both age 72 and retired and feel their joint life expectancy is approximately 15 years, they could withdraw from their account assuming a 25-year amortization period and a 5% interest rate. After the death of the surviving spouse, the designated beneficiaries would then withdraw the balance of the taxable IRA on a 10-year amortized basis. If the designated beneficiaries could reduce their income taxes by deferring the withdrawal of the balance of the taxable IRA until after they also retire, but within the 10-year window, they would obviously have this option under the RAP.

The major difference between the RAP and a plan of just taking RMDs is that, under the RAP, the withdrawals will be somewhat greater in the earlier years but significantly less in the later years, which in turn will hopefully create a smoothing out of taxable income at lower tax brackets. The goal of the RAP is to reduce the overall income tax rate at which the withdrawals will be taxed to the account owners by avoiding a large bunching of income during their working years as well as in the event they should outlive their life expectancies (when RMDs increase substantially), which will then result in a corresponding reduction in the income tax rates to the designated beneficiaries when they receive the balance of the taxable IRA payments during what are likely to be their peak earning years. During the account owners' lifetime the portion of the annual withdrawals under the RAP which exceeds the account owners' RMD amounts can be rolled into a Roth IRA, if desired.

2. Pay all or part of the IRA portion of the estate to lower-income-tax-bracket beneficiaries. The theory here is that, if we have to live with the new tax law, we can at least minimize its effects by planning our estates in a tax-sensitive manner. Assume, for example, that an individual has four children, two of whom are in high-income tax brackets and two who aren't. Why not consider leaving the IRA portion of the individual's estate to the children in lower brackets, and the assets with a stepped-up basis to the others? Of course, a drafting adjustment should be made for the fact that the lower-tax-bracket children will be receiving taxable income, whereas the others won't be. (See chapter VII.)

This plan can be taken a step further if the individual is interested in leaving a portion of his or her estate to grandchildren or great grandchildren, who may be in even lower income tax brackets than the children (subject to the so-called "Kiddie Tax" for grandchildren and great grandchildren as old as age 24). True, it's no longer possible to defer IRA income tax over the lives of these younger generations, but that does not mean it isn't helpful to distribute to grandchildren or great grandchildren (a group that's usually also larger in number than the older generation, thereby causing the income to be spread over more taxpayers). It's still a beneficial income tax planning technique because of the lower overall income taxes that often result.

An individual will also want to make any charitable gifts first out of the IRA portion of the estate, in effect turning income taxed at the highest rate into tax-free income.

3. Withdraw additional IRA funds early and use the after-tax amount to purchase income-tax-free life or long-term-care insurance. This option is intended to combine the RAP with option 2, above, but rather than convert all of the withdrawn funds under the RAP into Roth IRAs, the account owners invest all or a portion of the after-tax withdrawals in income-tax-free life insurance, including so-called second-to-die life insurance that pays only at the death of both spouses and is therefore cheaper than an individual policy insuring only one spouse.

The life insurance can then be left to the beneficiaries in the higher income tax brackets, while the remaining balance of the taxable IRA is distributed to beneficiaries in lower tax brackets, including, if desired, grandchildren and great grandchildren (again, of course with any adjustments desired to account for the disparate income tax treatment of the beneficiaries, and with due regard given for the potential application of the Kiddie Tax), and/or to charity.

Another option is to use the after-tax withdrawn funds under the RAP to purchase long-term-care insurance (including a hybrid life/long-term-care insurance policy) in order to protect the portion of the IRA that has not been withdrawn and potentially create an income tax deduction for premiums paid on a traditional long-term-care insurance policy (including a so-called "partnership program" traditional long-term-care insurance policy).

4. Pay IRA benefits to an income-tax-exempt charitable remainder trust. This alternative technique involves designating an income-tax-exempt charitable remainder trust as the beneficiary of the IRA proceeds. Assume, for example, that a $100 IRA is made payable to a charitable remainder unitrust that pays the owner's three children (ages 60, 58 and 56)—or pays the survivors or survivors of them—7.5% of the value of the trust corpus (determined annually) each year, until the last of the three children dies. Assume this takes 30 years, and that the trust grows at the same 7.5% annual rate throughout the 30 years. Under this plan, the owner's children will receive a total of $7.5 a year (or $5 after an assumed 33.3% combined federal and state ordinary income tax rate), which when then compounded outside of the trust, at a rate of 6% after a 20%

capital gains tax rate, will equal almost $400 in 30 years. The charity will receive the $100 principal at the end of the 30 years.

This sounds good, but compare this alternative to one of doing no planning. The $100 IRA would grow to $206 ten years after the owner's death. If we assume that there's a 40% tax rate on this amount (because of high tax rates during the children's peak earning years), this would net the children $124 upon withdrawal. Now assume the $124 grows at a 7.5% rate (or 6% net of an assumed 20% capital gains tax rate) for the next 20 years. Just as they would in the charitable trust alternative, the children would net almost $400. The major difference, however, is that the entirety of the IRA funds is available to the children, at all times, when the charitable remainder trust is not involved.

Paying IRA Funds to Trusts after the SECURE Act

After the death of the account owner, does it still make sense under the new law to pay funds from IRAs or 401Ks to trusts designed to protect the money for the beneficiary? (Traditionally, this has been done for protection against immaturity, lawsuits, divorce and estate taxes.) Many will argue it doesn't make sense anymore, because of the high income tax rates on trusts.

As discussed in chapters V and VII, however, you can handle those higher rates by judiciously using Section 678 of the Internal Revenue Code in the drafting of the trust. This allows the income of the trust to be taxed at the beneficiary's income tax rates, not the trust's rates. Note that this refers to the so-called "accumulation trust" approach to planning for payments from IRAs and other vehicles to trusts. It will not work in the case of a so-called "conduit trust," because conduit trusts mandate that all IRA and plan distributions be paid to the designated beneficiary of the trust upon receipt. Note also that existing "accumulation trusts" may need to be modified in light of the new law in order to ensure the 10-year deferral period for payments to a "designated beneficiary" is achieved over the 50% shorter five-year default period. The key language for the drafting attorney to focus on is found in the Code of Federal Regulations Section 1.401(a)(9)-4, A-1:

"A designated beneficiary need not be specified by name in the plan or by the employee to the plan in order to be a designated beneficiary so long as the individual who is to be the beneficiary is identifiable under the plan. The members of a class of beneficiaries capable of expansion or contraction will be treated as being identifiable if it possible to identify the class member with the shortest life expectancy." For example, if the trust includes a testamentary power of appointment to the surviving spouse of the beneficiary, with no age limit on the beneficiary's surviving spouse, the trust will not qualify as a designated beneficiary because it is impossible to identify the class member with the shortest life expectancy.

Which Technique is Best?

As will be discussed in the remaining chapters of this book, among all these strategies the ones that work best in a given situation will depend on all the facts and circumstances. The techniques can also be combined, if desired, to produce maximum benefits.

II

Use of Roth IRAs and Life Insurance after the SECURE Act

From a pre- and post-death income tax planning perspective, the SECURE Act is all about tax brackets. If left unaddressed the result of the new law will likely be that the account owners' children will be forced to pay income tax on the account owners' IRA balances at death over a maximum of 10 years—years in which the children are likely to already be in their peak tax brackets, e.g., ages 55 to 65.

The general recommendation for IRA and 401K account owners, once they retire (i.e., and are now in a low tax bracket), is for them to begin to "milk out" their IRA balances rather than (i) wait until age 72 to begin withdrawing their balances, and (ii) after attaining age 72, only withdraw the minimum required amounts each year—amounts which are typically very small until the account owners attain approximately age 85, when the tables are reversed. As introduced in chapter I, the concept behind the **"retirement amortization plan," or "RAP,"** is that retired account owners can minimize overall tax brackets for themselves and their children if they, in effect, "amortize" the IRAs over the lifetimes of the owners, plus 10 years thereafter (i.e., the children's maximum deferral period).

Take, for example, a recently retired couple ages 62 for the husband and 59 for the wife, who estimate their joint life expectancy to be 30 years. They then add 10 years onto this (for the distribution period of their children, under the SECURE Act), and attempt to amortize their IRAs equally over an approximate 40-year period.

Assume the couple's combined IRAs are worth $1,300,000. If the couple amortized this amount over 40 years, at a 5% interest rate, their annual withdrawals, as well as the total annual withdrawals of their children, would be approximately $75,000, which would keep the couple in the 12% tax bracket (under current law), even with other miscellaneous income included, and, more importantly, would minimize the income tax brackets of their children. Note also that the couple would enjoy the benefits of the "married filing jointly" income tax brackets and standard deduction, which is another reason to begin "milking out" IRA balances as soon as the couple is retired, and not wait until only one of the spouses may be living.

The above tax benefits of the RAP being rather obvious, the decision next becomes how to invest the $75,000 annual withdrawal. Prior to age 72, the couple could roll this entire annual amount into a Roth IRA. After attaining age 72, however, only the portion of the IRA withdrawal that exceeds the couple's required minimum distributions for the year can be converted into a Roth IRA.

For purposes of this analysis, we will assume the couple can roll the entire annual amount into a Roth IRA over their remaining 30-year combined life expectancy and/or invest it in assets which will produce no annual income, only appreciation, e.g., a non-dividend paying equity portfolio and/or tax-exempt bonds. After 30 years, compounded at a 5% rate of return, the $75,000 annual contributions would grow to $5,232,059. If either the husband or wife lives five years beyond their anticipated life expectancy, i.e., until age 97 for the husband and/or 94 for the wife, the $75,000 annual contributions would grow to approximately $7 million, again, all tax-free.

The couple's option would be to invest the $75,000 annual amount in income tax-free second-to-die life insurance, or one life insurance policy that does not pay out until both spouses die, and is therefore considerably less expensive than a policy on either spouse's life alone. Assuming the couple is in preferred health, the guaranteed income tax-free death benefit would be approximately $7 million.

The differences between the "Roth IRA investment plan" and the "second-to-die life insurance" investment plan are the following:

1. The Roth IRA investment plan is not guaranteed to produce the above-outlined tax-free results, which may be relevant to the couple in an unstable stock market.

2. Second-to-die life insurance is guaranteed, and obviously produces an income tax-free windfall for the children if the parents should die before the expiration of the 35 years. This windfall can then be utilized by the children to help pay the increased income taxes on the larger IRA receipts as a result of their not having been withdrawn during the couple's lifetime. This represents an advantage

of the second-to-die life insurance plan over the Roth IRA plan, i.e., in the event the couple should pass earlier than anticipated.

3. Unlike a Roth IRA, the cash value of the second-to-die policy will be small or non-existent if the goal is to maximize the income tax-free death benefit to the children, so clients who feel they may need to access a significant portion of the policy's cash surrender value during their lifetime will generally want to utilize a second-to-die life insurance policy with a smaller death benefit amount and a larger lifetime cash surrender value.

4. If the couple outlives the longer 35-year joint life expectancy referred to above, the Roth IRA approach would have then been preferable, in hindsight, assuming the 5% lifetime rate of return is achieved.

The couple could choose to hedge their bets and invest some of the $75,000 annual amount in a Roth IRA and some of it in second-to-die life insurance. The key point is that, either way, what the retired couple has accomplished by this plan is to minimize the effects of the potentially very high income tax brackets of their children (because likely the IRA balance will need to be paid out during the children's peak earnings years) by "milking out" their IRA balances during their retirement years and over their joint lifetime, at low tax rates, and transferring the withdrawn funds into a tax-free vehicle producing a reasonable rate of return.

Although beyond the scope of this handbook, if the death benefit of the life insurance is sufficient to cause federal or state estate taxes on the same, the couple will want to utilize an irrevocable life insurance trust to be the owner and beneficiary of the policy, in order to remove the policy's proceeds from the surviving spouse's taxable estate. The irrevocable trust can be drafted in a fashion which will allow the couple to access the cash surrender value of the policy during their lifetime, if necessary, without causing estate tax inclusion of the policy proceeds.[2]

Potential Limitations on the RAP

The RAP could apply equally to an unmarried retired account owner, of course utilizing a single-life policy rather than a survivorship policy. A relevant factor in deciding whether to employ the RAP for an unmarried individual, however, is a single individual's tax brackets and standard deduction versus the tax brackets and standard deduction of any married children of the account owner. To the extent being single causes the account owner to pay higher income taxes on the IRA or 401K distributions than his or her married children would pay, this of course should affect the amortization amount during the account owner's lifetime.

---

[2]For further information on this topic, please see the author's article entitled *The WRAP Trust*™, which can be found on the author's website, www.blaselaw.com. Please note, however, that the author has modified the actual drafting of the WRAP Trust over the years, the principal change being to utilize the conservative version of the trust, described in the article, coupled with a power in the insured grantor of the trust to replace an uncooperative trustee with another independent trustee.

Note also that the RAP will generally not apply to account owners who are living off of their IRAs or 401Ks or who plan to live off the same when they are retired. It likewise may not fully apply to account owners who are or will be receiving other pension plan distributions sufficient to cause them to be in a significant income tax bracket, since the goal of the RAP is to minimize overall income tax brackets for the account owners and the account owners' family.

III

Dueling Approaches to Roth Conversions after the SECURE Act

For years financial and tax advisors have counseled their clients to make Roth conversions when deemed expedient, but typically not to the extent the same pushes the client into a significantly higher federal income tax bracket. After the SECURE Act, does this strategy always still make tax sense?

Take, for example, this scenario: A couple, both age 65 and recently retired, have accumulated a combined taxable IRA of $2 million. They are expecting no other significant sources of retirement income, other than Social Security having a taxable portion assumed to be equal to their standard deduction amount. The couple estimates their current combined life expectancy at 20 years.

Especially given the likelihood of higher individual income tax rates beginning in the year 2026, if not earlier, common tax planning advice for this couple may be to withdraw taxable IRA funds earlier and to a greater extent than is required by the tax law, and then roll this amount (likely after tax, in this fact situation) either into a nontaxable Roth IRA, to the extent the amount withdrawn exceeds the required minimum distribution ("RMD") amount for the year, or into some other form of no-tax (e.g., life insurance or municipal bonds) or low-tax investments.

The question remains, however, what amount is the optimum annual amount to withdraw from the taxable IRA? There are two basic alternative approaches - the so-called "tax table approach," where the focus is on not causing the couple to be pushed into a significantly higher current income tax bracket, and the so-called "amortization table approach," which ignores current income tax brackets and instead focuses of lowering the total income tax liability of the couple and their children, after the couple's death.

Under the "tax table approach," the couple may choose to withdraw $80,250 per year (or about 4% of the initial IRA value) for the first seven years, because this will keep them in the 12% federal income tax bracket, and out of the 22% bracket (applying 2020 tax brackets). After that (i.e., age 72) the couple will be forced to take the larger RMDs. The federal income tax on the withdrawal during the first seven years (assuming the taxable portion of the couple's social security equals their standard deduction amount, and that their itemized deductions do not exceed their standard deduction) would be $9,235 per year, or $64,645 over the seven-year period, assuming tax rates do not change and the couple is able to file jointly the entire period. Assuming a 5 percent growth rate, the couple's taxable IRAs would be worth approximately $2.2 million after year seven. Again assuming a 5 percent growth rate, the total tax on the RMDs from year 8 through year 20 would be $215,343, for a total tax on the RMDs of $279,987 during the couple's estimated 20-year life expectancy.

Under the "amortization table approach," the couple would instead add their 20-year estimated life expectancy to the 10-year maximum period over which the couple's children must withdraw the balance of the taxable IRAs after the couple's death, and "amortize" their taxable IRAs over over 30 years. Assuming a 5 percent growth rate, equal annual withdrawals would be $128,837. The federal income tax on this larger amount would be $19,923 per year, or $398,478 over the couple's estimated 20-year life expectancy, again assuming tax rates do not change and the couple is able to file jointly the entire period. The couple thus pays $118,491 ($398,478 - $279,987) more in income taxes under the amortization table approach than under the tax table approach.

Under the amortization table approach, the amount remaining in the taxable IRAs at the couple's projected death in 20 years will be approximately $1 million; under the tax table approach the amount remaining in the taxable IRAs in 20 years will be approximately $2.2 million.

Now we need to compute the approximate annual withdrawal amount to the children after the couple's death, under each of the two approaches, assuming equal annual withdrawals over 10 years and a 5 percent growth rate. Under the 30-year amortization table approach, these annual withdrawals (on the approximately $1 million starting base) would be $127,279. Under the tax table approach, these annual withdrawals (on the approximately $2.2 million starting base) would be $280,013.

Now assume the couple has one child, and that this child's annual taxable income, excluding the equal IRA payments, but factoring in the child's standard deduction and itemized deductions, is $150,000. The child's total annual taxable income during the 10-year payout period would be $277,279 under the amortization table approach and $430,013 under the tax table approach.

Assuming 2020 tax tables and that the child's tax status is married filing jointly (and ignoring for this purpose any potential tax on Social Security payments), the child's annual tax liability would be $54,706 under the amortization table approach (and $547,060 total, over 10 years) and $100,094 under the tax table approach (and $1,000,940 total, over 10 years), a difference of $453,880 over 10 years. This amount must then be compared to the $118,491 lower lifetime tax amount of the tax table approach versus the amortization table approach, for a net tax savings in favor of the amortization table approach over the tax table approach, over the entire 30 years, of $335,389. This tax savings could be even larger if the child was in a higher income tax bracket.

It can be argued that, while this tax savings in favor of the tax amortization table approach is substantial, it does not reflect the time value of the loss use of the $118,491additional tax payments during the lifetime of the couple. However, this potential loss in the time value of money must be balanced against the potential that one of the two spouses will die some years before the other, so by not withdrawing the additional amount earlier, when the couple's tax bracket was essentially half the tax bracket of the widow or widower, these two competing factors can be viewed as essentially cancelling each other out. Also remember tax rates could rise in the future, so withdrawing a larger amount earlier may also be beneficial from this perspective.

The numbers can obviously be run a variety of ways, and of course there are countless different client fact patterns. The purpose of this chapter is merely to illustrate that traditional Roth conversions strategies need to be challenged in light of the SECURE Act, to ensure that families are not foregoing a significant potential family income tax savings by not exploring all of the Roth conversions approaches available to them.

IV

A Tax-Smart IRA and 401K Beneficiary Plan for the SECURE Act

The two-fold concern created by the new tax law is that not only must all of the tax on IRA and 401K benefits be paid much earlier than in the past, but the tax rate on the receipts will likely be much higher than in the past, due to the bunching of income during a period when the recipients are likely to be in their peak earning years, e.g., ages 55 through 65.

There are a number of alternatives the client can consider in order to mitigate the adverse effects of the new tax law. One idea is to pay all or part of the IRA or 401K portion of the owner's estate to significantly lower income tax bracket beneficiaries. The theory here is that, if we have to live with the new tax law, at least minimize its effects by planning our estates in a tax wise manner.

Assume, for example, that an individual has four children, two in high income tax brackets and two in low. Why not consider leaving the IRA portion of the individual's estate to the children in low income tax brackets, with the other, income tax-free assets, to the children in the high tax brackets? Of course, a compensating drafting adjustment (i.e., via specific cash gifts) should be made for the fact that the low tax bracket children will be receiving taxable income (probably in a higher tax bracket than they were previously), whereas the others will not be. If more than one child will be receiving a portion of the IRA, the compensating adjustments should factor in the relative tax brackets of all children receiving a portion of the IRA (at their anticipated new tax brackets), as well as their relative percentage interests in the IRA receipts.

The children's relative percentage interests in the IRA portion of the individual's estate, as well as the amount of any compensating adjustments, may obviously need to be changed over time, depending on all relevant future facts and circumstances, including all children's anticipated future income tax situations, anticipated retirement ages, etc. This analysis will become part of the individual's regular periodic update of his or her estate plan over time.

This plan can be taken a step further if the individual is interested in leaving a portion of his or her estate to grandchildren and/or great grandchildren, who may be in even lower income tax brackets than the lower tax bracket children (subject, again, to the so-called "Kiddie Tax"). Just because an existing plan to defer income tax on IRA assets over the lifetime of grandchildren and/or great grandchildren will no longer be possible, does not mean distributions to grandchildren and/or great grandchildren in lower tax brackets (and who are usually also more in number than children, thus spreading the IRA, etc. income over more taxpayers) is not still a beneficial income tax planning strategy, due to the lower overall income taxes which may result.

To illustrate the potential benefits involved with this tax-wise IRA planning technique, assume that an individual has two children, A (in a 20% combined federal and state income tax bracket) and B (in a 40% combined federal and state income tax bracket), and an estate consisting of a $1 million IRA and $1.5 million in cash, investments, real estate and life insurance proceeds passing outside of the IRA. Instead of leaving the IRA equally to A and B, the individual might decide instead to leave the $1 million IRA all to child A, with the cash, investments, real estate and life insurance held outside of the IRA split equally under the individual's estate planning documents between the two children, after adjusting for the IRA passing to child A outside of the individual's estate planning documents. The individual might then elect to make a specific cash gift to child A of $200,000, in order to compensate A for the income taxes A will need to pay on the $1 million IRA.

Based on the aforesaid assumptions, the individual's $2,500,000 total assets would be distributed as follows:

a. Child A would receive: (1) the $1 million IRA passing outside of the individual's estate planning documents; (2) the $200,000 cash gift the individual elected to leave A to compensate for the income taxes A will pay on the IRA distributions; and (3) $150,000 cash, investments, real estate and life insurance, or $1,350,000 total; and

b. Child B would receive $1,150,000 cash, investments, real estate and life insurance, with no benefits under the IRA, and no compensating adjustment since B will not be paying taxes on IRA distributions.

On an after-tax basis, A receives 800K worth of IRA plus 350K [i.e., 200K + 150K] worth of cash, investments, real estate and life insurance, or $1,150,000, total, net of taxes. Had there been no tax planning, A would have received $1,150,000, net of taxes, so A's situation remains the same.

B, on the other hand, now receives $1,150,000, income tax free, or $100,000 more than B would have received, net of taxes, had there been no tax planning [i.e., $750,000 cash, investments, real estate and life insurance, plus $300,000 after-tax value of one-half interest in IRA].

Each child receives an identical amount, net of taxes, and the family as a whole comes out $100,000 ahead. These tax advantages could obviously be even greater if the IRA were left to grandchildren or great grandchildren in lower tax brackets, subject to the potential application of the so-called "Kiddie Tax."

The above-outlined plan has the additional benefit of essentially treating the new tax law as an estate tax on the individual's estate. Most individuals wish for their assets to pass equally to their children at their deaths, after all taxes. The above tax-wise IRA beneficiary plan helps carry out this intent, saving the family significant tax dollars, in the process.

V

Paying IRAs and 401Ks to Trusts; Examining Ed Slott's New Stretch IRA

Ed Slott's articles in response to the SECURE Act, while well-intended, contain too many overgeneralizations regarding estate planning. Let's take his February 6, 2020 online article in *Financial Planning*, for example: "Why Life Insurance Is The New Stretch IRA."

The article's initial premise is certainly correct: "Clients [with the largest IRA balances] are naturally concerned about post-death control. They built large IRAs and want to make sure that these funds are not misused, lost or squandered by beneficiaries due to mismanagement, lawsuits, divorce, bankruptcy or by falling prey to financial scams or predators." Unfortunately, from this point on the article succumbs to several overgeneralizations regarding estate planning with IRAs, and the use of trusts.

In the first place, life insurance is not the new stretch IRA. As already illustrated in this book, life insurance has always played an important role in tax and estate planning for IRAs, but it is *not* the "new stretch IRA." Individuals should not be mislead into thinking it is.

The article suggests: "In order to keep your client's IRA estate plan intact, the IRA portion will probably have to be replaced with either a Roth IRA (via lifetime Roth conversions) or with life insurance, which offers better leverage and flexibility since it won't be subject to any post-death SECURE Act limitations." "Replaced?" So the goal is to completely replace (i.e., with life insurance or Roth IRAs) the IRA portion of the estates of clients "with the largest IRA balances?"

Although, as discussed in chapter II, it is definitely recommended that retired individuals consider annually "milking out" a portion of their IRAs, at lower income tax rates, and rolling the after-tax proceeds into life insurance and/or, in the case of the portion of the withdrawal over the required minimum distribution for the year, a Roth IRA, the advisor must be very careful before embarking on a program to completely replace "the largest IRA balances" in this fashion, without first carefully examining the after-tax math associated with each individual plan.

The article also suggests cashing out IRAs, paying income taxes, now, at potentially significant income tax rates, and then using the after-tax proceeds to purchase life insurance for grandchildren. Remember that these same grandchildren are likely to be in lower income tax brackets than their grandparents at the time of the liquidation of the taxable IRAs. If we are using the after-tax IRA proceeds to purchase tax-free life insurance (which, again, can be an effective tax-saving strategy), then why do we need to leave the life insurance proceeds to grandchildren, when we were only using them for their longer life expectancies (which now have become moot), in the first place?

If we are primarily using grandchildren for the income tax leverage that they bring to the table, why don't the same grandchildren bring income tax leverage for IRAs after the SECURE Act? Remember, these grandchildren are likely to be in lower income tax brackets than the IRA owners doing the liquidating of the largest IRA balances, and, more importantly, they are likely to be more numerous than one IRA owner, thus spreading the taxable IRA proceeds over many more taxpayers.

The article continues:

"Under the old stretch IRA rules, if the trust qualified as a see-through trust, RMDs could be based on the age of the oldest grandchild, say, a 19-year-old. RMDs would be paid to the trust and from the trust right through to the individual grandchildren over 64 years (the life expectancy for a 19-year-old), leaving the bulk of the inherited IRA funds protected in trust for decades…"

"But no more. Under the SECURE Act, if this plan stays as is, all of the funds will be released to the grandchildren and taxed by the end of the 10th year after death—contrary to the client's intention. Even if a discretionary (accumulation) trust was used to keep more funds protected, the entire inherited IRA balance would still have to be paid out to the trust by the end of the 10 years—and be taxed at trust rates for any funds retained in the trust for continued protection."

Let's unpack these two paragraphs to see if they are accurate.

In the first place, subject to the potential application of the so-called "Kiddie Tax," why would it be a bad idea to pay IRA benefits to a trust for a grandchild in his or her early working years? Aren't these the years when the grandchild will likely be in his or her lowest income tax brackets? Are we sure it makes sense for an IRA owner to withdraw funds prior to retirement, at a likely higher income tax rate than the grandchildren will be in, only to pay these higher income taxes on the IRA proceeds many years before it would otherwise be necessary? It might be wise to run the after-tax math on this idea, first, and in so doing factor in the number of grandchildren (i.e., separate taxpayers) involved, versus the lone IRA owner-taxpayer.

The two paragraphs then suggest that, under the SECURE Act, all of the funds of the trust will be released to the grandchildren and taxed by the end of the 10th year after death. This is an incorrect statement. The SECURE Act does not require that the funds be released to the grandchildren by the end of the 10th year after death, or indeed at any point. The client may choose to release the funds to the grandchildren by this point, but the SECURE Act itself does not require this.

Finally, these two paragraphs conclude that if a discretionary (accumulation) trust was used to keep more funds protected, the funds would "be taxed at trust rates for any funds retained in the trust for continued protection." This overgeneralization about the trust income tax laws is not true. As discussed in detail in chapter VII, the beneficiary can be given a power of withdrawal over the IRA proceeds payable to the trust and the proceeds will be taxed at the individual's income tax rates, and not at the trust's income tax rates, regardless of whether the beneficiary actually withdraws the proceeds from the trust.

The article continues: "Due to the life insurance leverage, the payout after death can far exceed the $1 million balance in the IRA, of course depending on the client's age and health." This is a true statement, if it is referring to the "after tax" payout. But this has always been the case when life insurance proceeds are compared to IRA proceeds; there is nothing new about the SECURE Act which leads us to this conclusion regarding the potential income tax benefits of life insurance.

Finally, the article suggests: "Life insurance trusts can be more versatile for multi-generational planning as well, keeping the funds protected for decades if desired." Again, this is an overgeneralization of state law and the federal income tax laws. Under most state laws and the federal income tax law trusts receiving IRA proceeds can be protected for generations, just as life insurance trusts can be.

Ed Slott's articles are based on a misconception of the federal income tax laws applicable to trusts as well as the asset protection laws applicable in most states. Take this assertion Mr. Slott makes in his article appearing in the January 7, 2020 online edition of *Financial Planning*, "New Tax Law Obliterates IRA Trust Planning":

"With a discretionary trust, when more post-death control is desired, the annual RMDs are paid out from the inherited IRA to the trust, but then the trustee has discretion over whether to distribute those funds to the trust beneficiaries or retain them in the trust. This provides the trustee with greater post-death control of what gets paid to the trust beneficiaries, as compared to the conduit trust, which pays out all annual RMDs to the trust beneficiaries. *Any funds retained in the trust though would be taxed at high trust tax rates.*" (Emphasis added.)

The statement, "Any funds retained in the trust though would be taxed at high trust tax rates," is an overgeneralization about how trusts are taxed for federal income tax purposes. Again as discussed further in chapter VII, properly drafted trusts will grant the beneficiary a power of withdrawal over the trust income, subject to a suspension power in the trustee in the event the beneficiary is abusing the withdrawal power or in the event of a creditor attack against the trust. Drafted in this manner, the trust does not even pay income taxes. All of the trust income is taxed to the beneficiary, at the beneficiary's income tax rates. Furthermore, the trust income that is not withdrawn during the year accumulates inside the trust, and in most states remains protected for the beneficiary, which, as mentioned at the outset of this article, was Mr. Slott's initial and correct premise for writing his articles.

As discussed in chapter II and throughout this book, no doubt life insurance is an important tool in an individual's arsenal of tools intended to counteract the punitive effects of the SECURE Act, but it is not the new stretch IRA. Equally important are the various other tools discussed in this book which the individual can utilize to help minimize the income tax liability on the IRA proceeds themselves.

VI

Postmortem Tax Planning for IRA and 401K Distributions after the SECURE Act

The SECURE Act has changed the way certain beneficiaries[3] will need to think about receiving their IRA and 401K benefits. Previously these beneficiaries had their whole lives to remove that money. Now they have to do it 10 years, and these more concentrated distributions from IRAs and 401Ks could throw them into higher tax brackets.

The new law means that IRA and 401K beneficiaries and their advisors will need to be on the alert after the IRA or 401K participant/owner passes. The individual's estate planning file—especially his or her home or safekeeping file—needs to be carefully flagged with a bold notation for the beneficiaries to seek the advice of a competent tax advisor before they make any decisions about the withdrawal of funds from IRAs and qualified plans after the participant/owner's passing.

Let's assume, for example, that the participant/owner dies when his or her three children range in age from 55 to 63. Under this likely common scenario, how should the

---

[3]Note that, as described in chapter VI, these rules do not apply to surviving spouses and certain other types of beneficiaries.

children be advised if they would like to minimize the otherwise harsh effects of the SECURE Act?

The key factor will be tax brackets. Assume, for example, that the 63-year-old child is two years from retirement. It's very likely, then, that it will be wise for this child to defer taking any distribution for two years when the child is still making income (and when extra income from an IRA can pump up the child's tax bracket). After retirement, the now-65-year-old would take one-eighth of the IRA's distribution per year.

Now let's take the 55-year-old child. Assume that this child is "about 10 years" from retirement. It's very likely then, that it will make sense for this child to the spread the IRA proceeds equally over the entire 10-year period.

If a child is not yet on Social Security or Medicare, it may make sense to accelerate the payments. That way, a lesser amount of the child's future Social Security payments will be taxed (in some states, those benefits can be taxed at the state level as well). Also, the smaller payments will have less effect on future Part B Medicare premiums; in other words, it won't push them up. Bear in mind, however, that for Medicare Part B purposes there is a "two-year lag" in the reported income figures that the government uses for these computations.

If a child has children of his own who may be in their early working years (and not subject to the so-called Kiddie Tax), it may make sense for the child to disclaim all or a portion of the IRA proceeds so that they will then be spread among more taxpayers—taxpayers who are likely to be in lower income tax brackets than the child who would otherwise receive the proceeds.

Finally, if a "minor" child or trust for a minor child is a beneficiary of an IRA or 401K, it may make sense for the child or trust to take distributions *more* rapidly than the law requires, because of the child's lower income tax bracket at the time versus what it may be in the future, again subject to the potential application of the Kiddie Tax if either or both of the child's parents is/are then living. [See the discussion of the new "eligible designated beneficiary" rules as applied to a minor child, at page 86.]

The postmortem planning point eventually becomes self-evident: With the advent of the new accelerated distribution rules for IRAs and other qualified plans, the beneficiaries need to shrewdly examine all of their options for withdrawing the proceeds if they want to minimize their total income tax liability on the distributions.

VII

Trust Drafting Recommendations

The disparate federal income tax treatment between trusts and individuals, that has existed since 1986, has grown even more pronounced with the passage of the 2017 and 2019 (SECURE Act) year-end tax laws. This chapter will examine the problems which currently face us and will propose solutions to these problems.

Impact of the 2017 Year-End Tax Changes

As a result of the 2017 year-end tax changes, structuring trusts for spouses, descendants and other beneficiaries, in a fashion which minimizes the aggregate federal income tax liability for the trust and its beneficiaries, has become more important than ever. Discussed below are some of the reasons why:

In 2020 individuals can effectively exclude the first $12,400 ($24,800, if married) of income, whereas trusts can effectively exclude only the first $100 ($300, if a simple trust). Individuals are also taxed at significantly lower ordinary income tax rates than trusts at the same level of taxable income. This disparate income tax treatment has widened considerably as a result of the 2017 tax changes.

For example, an individual with $172,925 of interest income, and no deductions, paid $32,748.50 of federal income tax in 2019, while married couples with the same level of interest income paid only $24,392.50 of federal income tax in 2019. Complex trusts with the same amount of interest income, and no deductions (including the distribution deduction), on the other hand, paid $68,389.90 of federal income tax in 2019 [$62,303.25 regular tax + $6,086.65 net investment income tax]. These differences under the new tax law are obviously staggering. A trust pays well over twice as much federal income tax as a single individual with the same amount of interest income, and almost three times as much as a married couple with the same amount.

For comparison purposes, before the 2017 year-end tax changes a single individual with the same amount of interest income paid $38,488.75 of federal tax in 2017, and a married couple paid $29,508.75. A complex trust paid $73,714 in 2017. Thus, utilizing the above example, as a result of the 2017 year-end tax changes the single individual's federal taxes went down 17.5% while the married couple's federal taxes went down 21%. Complex trusts, on the other hand, saw their taxes go down by only 7.8%. Simply put, this means that the relative disparity between trust income tax treatment and individual income tax treatment grew even greater as a result of the 2017 year-end tax changes. If the same trust income were instead spread between or among two or more children beneficiaries of the trust, the disparity between the trust and individual income tax brackets would become even more apparent.

Individuals also enjoy a substantial benefit over trusts when it comes to the income taxation of capital gains and qualified dividends. A trust may only have $2,900 (in 2020) of taxable income and still be taxed at 0% on its capital gains and qualified dividends. The comparable level for single individuals is almost 14 times higher, or $40,000 (in 2020, assuming the individual has no other income), which, when combined with the single beneficiary's $12,400 standard deduction, means that a single individual (including a minor child) could have up to $52,400 in qualified dividends, annually, without paying any federal income tax, subject to the potential application of the Kiddie Tax rules. [See IRC Section 1(h)(1)(B).] A trust with a like amount of qualified dividend income, on the other hand, would pay approximately $10,750 in income tax (applying 2018 rates), including approximately $1,500 in net investment income tax. The same annual amount compounded at 4%, over 20 years, would equal approximately $320,000, which can certainly help pay for college.

A similar but more dramatic result would occur if there were two or more beneficiaries of the trust. As long as each beneficiary's taxable income was less than $52,400, they would each pay no federal income tax on the capital gains and qualified dividends. Thus, there could be over $150,000 of qualified dividends and capital gains inside of a trust, which if taxed equally to three single individual beneficiaries, with no independent income of their own, would result in $0 federal income tax. The annual federal income tax to the trust, on the other hand, including the net investment income tax, would be approximately $34,000 (applying 2018 tax rates). Compounded annually at 4% over

20 years again, this annual income tax difference would equal over $1 million!

Similar larger tax gaps between trusts and individuals occur at the 15% and 20% capital gain rates, as well as at ordinary income tax rates.

Trusts also pay the 3.8% net investment income tax on the lesser of undistributed net investment income or adjusted gross income in excess of $12,750 (for 2019); a single individual, on the other hand, needs to have net investment income or modified AGI in excess of $200,000 ($250,000 for married couples) before he or she will pay the 3.8% tax.

The singular tax benefit trusts now maintain over individuals is the deduction for trustee fees, trust tax return preparation fees, and other expenses uniquely related to trusts. Trusts are entitled to these deductions whereas individuals are not.

Given that most income generated by trusts is passive income, it is extremely important for CPAs, estate planning attorneys, trustees and their financial advisors to be aware of the significant disparity in the federal income taxation of the various types of passive income taxable to trusts versus individuals, whether that be in tax planning, document preparation, encroachment decisions, or investment decisions. The client's professional team also needs to be ever-cognizant of the non-tax advantages of retaining income and capital gains inside trusts when it comes to estate tax protection, divorce protection, creditor protection, and the various protections which are normally associated with underage and otherwise financially immature beneficiaries. These significant advantages of trusts would all be negated to the extent the trustee chooses to distribute the income (including qualified plan and IRA receipts) and capital gains to the beneficiary in an effort to plan around the severely compressed trust income and capital gains tax brackets.

It would be a simple matter to distribute all of the current income of the trust to the trust beneficiaries, in order to avoid the compressed trust income tax rates. In limited circumstances (e.g., by allocating capital gains to trust accounting income in the trust document), it might also be possible to distribute the trust's capital gains to the beneficiaries, in order to avoid the higher capital gains rates typically applicable to trusts, as well as the 3.8% net investment income tax.

The problem is that few clients want these automatic trust distributions to their children or other heirs to occur. For the parents of minors and other young children and adults, the issue is obvious. Parents of young children and adults do not want significant automatic annual distributions to the children, or to the guardian or conservator for the children, to be made. Parents of older children are more concerned with issues of divorce protection, creditor protection, and estate tax minimization (including state death taxes) for their children.

The automatic distribution of trust income and capital gains to the children ignores this legitimate parental concern. Parents of special needs children also obviously do not want the trust income to be paid to the children.

Drafting Solutions

Here are some planning thoughts which the trustee or advisor may wish to consider to assist clients in responding to their predicament - the challenge of achieving significant income tax savings while also preserving the non-tax purposes of the trust.

Use of §678 Withdrawal Power Over Trust Income

For new trusts, drafting an IRC Section 678(a)(1) withdrawal power over trust accounting income into the trust (other than a simple trust), in order to tax the trust beneficiary on all trust taxable income, is not only permissible in the tax law, but, for all the income-tax-saving reasons outlined above, is usually advisable. [See Regs. §§1.678(a)-1, 1.671-3(c), 1.677(a)-1(g), Ex. 2.]

This withdrawal power should be coupled with a power in the trustee to allocate capital gains and IRA, etc. receipts to trust accounting income pursuant to a reasonable and impartial (i.e., with respect to current and remainder beneficiaries, including permissible appointees and takers in default of appointment) exercise of a discretionary power in the governing instrument, factoring in tax consequences to the trust and its beneficiaries. [*See* Regs. §1.643(b)-1] Inclusion of the "reasonable and impartial" standard (which is actually already a part of most states' "duty of impartiality" for trustees) should forestall an IRS argument that a trustee-beneficiary possesses a general power of appointment over the entirety of the IRA, etc. accounts and the appreciation portion of the securities as a result of the withdrawal power over trust accounting income.

The withdrawal power should also include a power in the trustee to fully or partially suspend the beneficiary's future withdrawal power in appropriate situations, e.g., immature or unwise use of withdrawn funds by the beneficiary, lawsuits, divorce, college financial aid qualification reasons, or, as discussed below, for the purpose of minimizing overall income taxes to the trust and its beneficiaries.

Except in the case where IRAs, etc., are distributable to the trust (which situation is discussed later in this chapter), it may even be possible, and make sense in some circumstances, to add a Section 678 withdrawal power to a "special" or "supplemental" needs trust, e.g., by giving the withdrawal power to a sibling or siblings in a modest income tax bracket. If so, the sibling's withdrawal power would again want to be coupled with an ability in the trustee to suspend the same, if the sibling is not acting in the special needs child's best interests. (See the additional discussion on trustee suspension powers, below.)

Note that if the withdrawal power holder needs funds to pay the income tax attributable to his or withdrawal right, he or she merely may exercise the withdrawal power to the extent so necessary. An alternative would be to allow an independent trustee to pay these taxes, either directly or indirectly by reimbursing the beneficiary.

Some may argue that a minor's legal guardian has a fiduciary duty to exercise the Section 678 withdrawal power on behalf of the ward/beneficiary, and that therefore employment of the power of withdrawal in the case of minor beneficiaries could turn out to defeat the parents' desire that their children do not receive substantial sums at age 18. Is this a sound argument? Would a legal guardian, knowing that any amounts not withdrawn on the beneficiary's behalf will remain in a creditor-protected trust held exclusively for the ward's benefit, and that the ward will eventually control this trust at a designated age, be acting in the ward's best interest if he or she chose to exercise the withdrawal power and deposit the withdrawn funds in an unprotected guardianship or conservatorship account for the ward?

Assume the ward is later involved in a major car accident, and the guardianship or conservatorship estate is exhausted to satisfy a claim against the ward. Could the guardian then be surcharged for foolishly and needlessly withdrawing the funds from the protected trust? The point is self-evident. Regardless, as discussed in the immediately below section titled "Use of Trustee Suspension Power," the trustee could merely threaten to suspend the beneficiary's withdrawal power should the trustee determine the exercise of the same by a guardian acting on behalf of a minor would needlessly expose the protected trust assets to lawsuits.

Some may also argue that, under IRC Section 678(a)(2) and IRS private letter rulings, when the beneficiary's withdrawal power lapses each year, the beneficiary continues to be taxed on an ever-increasing portion of the trust's income, including capital gains. The problem with this argument (aside from the fact that it is really just an argument in favor of lower income taxes, in most instances) is that it flies in the face of the Internal Revenue Code itself, as the withdrawal power holder has not "partially released or otherwise modified" the power. The power lapses by the terms of the trust, not by any affirmative "release" or "modification" on the part of the beneficiary withdrawal power holder, which is what Section 678(a)(2) requires. In any event, because it is now normally desired that all of the trust's taxable income be taxable to the current beneficiary anyway, this debate is now largely moot.

Because the beneficiary's withdrawal right is designed to fully or partially (i.e., subject to a "hanging power") lapse at the end of each year, i.e., to the extent of 5% of the value of the trust each year, in order avoid annual taxable gifts under IRC Section 2514(e), will the lapsed amount be accessible to the beneficiary's future creditors? In most states, and under the Uniform Trust Code, the beneficiary's annual power (including, presumably, any "hanging power") is not protected, but the annual lapses of the withdrawal rights, are. [The American College of Trust & Estate Counsel, or ACTEC, has an excellent web link on this topic.] In the balance of the states which do not protect the annual lapse of the withdrawal right from the beneficiary's creditors the question must be asked: Who is the real "creditor" here, when the alternative to "Section 678 planning" is to pay much higher income taxes to the IRS?

While the beneficiaries of a trust can protect themselves against many types of potential future lawsuits with umbrella liability insurance, these policies will obviously be ineffective as against the excessive income taxes the trust will most certainly owe the IRS.

Use of Trustee Suspension Power

With the current and future uncertainty in the tax law, with the uncertainty in the trust's and beneficiary's respective tax situations, and with the above-described varied treatment of the Section 678 withdrawal power for creditor rights purposes, the Section 678 power needs to be drafted in a flexible fashion, so that it can adapt to various and changing circumstances. One way of accomplishing this is to allow an "independent trustee" (meaning one with no beneficial interest in the trust) the opportunity to either (i) annually suspend (and restore), broaden and/or alter future withdrawal powers, in whole or in part, prior to January 1 of the next tax year, or (ii) amend the trust's terms to achieve the lowest combined current income tax liability for the trust and its beneficiaries, but without affecting existing withdrawal powers. [See *Blattmachr on Income Taxation of Estates and Trusts* §5.5.1 (Seventeenth Edition 2018).]

Another reason for the needed flexibility is the above-alluded-to manner in which certain trust expenses are treated for trust versus individual income tax purposes. The unbundled portion of trustee fees not attributable to investment advisory services, for example, may be deductible for trust income tax purposes, under the current tax law, but not deductible for individual income tax purposes. Under the IRS Regulations, an allocable portion of these types of fees would be applied to the beneficiary of the Section 678 withdrawal power, and as a consequence would no longer be deductible. [*See* Regs. §§1.678(a)-1, 1.671-3(c), 1.677(a)-1(g), Ex. 2.] The trustee may thus find itself in a situation where the federal marginal income tax rate applicable to the individual beneficiary is much lower than the federal marginal income tax rate applicable to the trust, but making use of the individual's income tax rate would eliminate a potentially significant annual income tax deduction.

Take, for example, a $2 million trust with a 1% annual trustee fee on the first $1 million of assets and a 0.75% fee on the next million. The total annual trustee fee would be $17,500. Assume also that no portion of this fee is allocable to tax-exempt income. If the deduction for this fee is lost by allocating it to the individual beneficiary under a Section 678 power, the negative annual income tax effect could be as much as $6,500. If the individual beneficiary is at least that much ahead by having the trust income and capital gains taxed to him or her, versus the trust, this may be fine; but if the overall savings is less than this, suspension of the beneficiary's Section 678 withdrawal power by an independent trustee may be in order. In most cases this will be easy enough to do, because the trust would likely already have an independent trustee in place. Note also that, after the suspension, the independent trustee will still retain the power to make IRC Sections 661/662 distributions to the individual beneficiary with the "after tax deduction income," the negative, of course, being the loss of the non-tax advantages for retaining assets in trust.

Suspension or alteration of the individual beneficiary's future withdrawal powers may likewise be advantageous when the trust would otherwise be entitled to a significant tax deduction for state taxes paid (if state capital gains taxes would otherwise be payable by the trust as a result of a large capital gain inside the trust), at a time when the individual beneficiary is already benefitting from a similar state tax deduction. Suspending the individual beneficiary's future Section 678 withdrawal power may make it possible to, in effect, "double up" on the current $10,000 annual ceiling on the state income tax deduction and achieve an aggregate deduction of as much as $20,000.

As in the case of the trustee fee deduction, this technique could then be coupled with an IRC Sections 661/662 distribution to the individual beneficiary of the "after tax deduction income." Again, the aggregate tax savings of using the suspension power in this situation should be balanced against the non-tax reasons for retaining the income in the trust. Note too that, under the trustee standard for determining trust accounting income described at page 40, the trustee need not allocate all capital gains and IRA, etc. receipts to withdrawable trust accounting income, thus leaving some of this gross income in the trust to absorb "trust only" deductions. Under either planning technique, remember that the grantor trust "portion rules" under Section 1.671-3 of the Regulations do not allow for a dollar-for-dollar tax deduction by the trust; a portion of the deductions will be allocated to the beneficiary and not be deductible on the trust tax return, in any event.

Suspension of the individual beneficiary's future Section 678 withdrawal power may also make sense if the individual beneficiary is already in a high tax bracket, or if the individual beneficiary is subject to the so-called "Kiddie Tax" in a particular year. However, before making this decision, the independent trustee should bear in mind that this type of individual beneficiary might also be benefiting on the estate tax side, by personally paying the income taxes attributable to an estate or generation-skipping transfer tax exempt trust's income. If the decision to suspend is made here, remember that the independent trustee can always restore the beneficiary's withdrawal power in the future, in full or in part, if and when changed circumstances dictate.

In certain situations it may make sense for an independent trustee to only partially suspend a beneficiary's future Section 678 withdrawal power. For example, if the trust does not have any significant tax deductions which would be lost, it might be beneficial to suspend the beneficiary's withdrawal power only over an amount equal to the level at which the trust reaches the maximum income tax bracket (e.g., $12,951 in 2020), or to some other lower tax bracket level. In so doing, the trustee may also elect to limit the suspension to income items other than qualified dividends and capital gains, first, so that the beneficiary may avail himself or herself of the significantly larger 0% tax bracket amount for these items, while also avoiding the 3.8% tax on net investment income.

Bear in mind, however, that the tax benefits of this "partial" suspension will be limited by the fact that the general effective tax rate on the compressed lower brackets of the trust is over 24%, a rate which does not kick in for single individuals until income levels of almost $98,000 (in 2020, including the $12,400 standard deduction). [The married couple numbers are twice these figures.] The next tax bracket of 32% is not reached until the single individual has over $175,700 in income, including the $12,400 standard deduction. [Again, the married couple numbers are twice these figures.] Thus, unless the beneficiary has a significant taxable income, utilizing this partial suspension technique will normally be tax neutral, at best. In fact, and as alluded to above, subject to the potential application of the Kiddie Tax rules, if the beneficiary has little or no separate income, utilizing the suspension technique may effectively cause some loss of the 0% tax rate on qualified dividends and capital gains to a single beneficiary with income (including the $12,400 standard deduction) of $52,400 or less in 2020.

As alluded to above, perhaps the most important reason for including a trustee suspension power in the trust is that it allows the trustee to maintain some control over the beneficiary's "non-tax situation." This is what concerns parents the most. As just some of the potential examples, the trustee might suspend the beneficiary's future withdrawal power (i) because of the immature or unwise use of funds the beneficiary is withdrawing from the trust, (ii) to motivate the beneficiary to take a particular action (e.g., go to college, or get a job), (iii) because the beneficiary is getting a divorce, (iv) because the beneficiary is involved in a lawsuit, or (v) because the beneficiary is attempting to qualify for college financial aid and a withdrawal right would hinder these efforts.

Due to the multitude and potential complexity of the issues involved, the trust document should exonerate the independent trustee for any decision or non-decision relative to the trustee's suspension power. The trustee should also be reminded that, in order to clearly comply with the IRC Section 678(a)(1) requirements, the suspension power may only be exercised effective January 1 of the following tax year. This will typically require some level of annual dialogue between or among the trust's CPA, attorney, trustee and/or investment advisor.

Trust Income Which Exceeds the §2514(e) Limitation

Assume that a significant portion of the trust accounting income (including capital gains and IRA, etc., receipts allocated to trust accounting income) would exceed the Section 2514(e) 5% limitation. Is there a solution to this problem which will cause the beneficiary to be taxed on the income, but without the potential of causing a taxable lapse under either IRC Section 2041(b)(2) or 2514(e)?

There is a 9th Circuit Court of Appeals decision, *Fish v. United States*, 432 F.2d 1278 (9th Cir. 1970), which, although incorrectly decided, nevertheless stands for the proposition that the "5 and 5" limitation in the case of a beneficiary's withdrawal power over income can only be based on the current income of the trust as the denominator. It cannot be based on the entire value of the trust, even if the trustee is expressly granted the power, under the trust instrument, to use any assets of the trust in order to satisfy the beneficiary's exercise of the withdrawal power. The court's theory was that, because the beneficiary possessed no withdrawal power over trust principal, the latter could not be included in the "5% denominator," despite the clear language of the Internal Revenue Code to the contrary if the trustee was permitted to use any asset of the trust to satisfy the exercise of the beneficiary's withdrawal power.

Therefore, if we wish to "stay clear" of *Fish*, and simultaneously cause all of the trust's current income (including capital gains and IRA, etc., distributions) to be taxed to the trust's beneficiary, and not to the trust, we need to utilize the following three-step process:

Step 1: Provide in the trust document that the trust's current beneficiary has a right to withdraw all of the current income of the trust, including, as defined in the trust document, all capital gains and IRA, etc., distributions.

Step 2: Provide in the trust document that the beneficiary's withdrawal power over this trust income lapses at the end of each year, but only to the extent it will not constitute a release under either IRC Section 2041(b)(2) or 2514(e), and make clear in the trust document that the trustee can use any of the trust's assets, whether current income or principal, to satisfy the exercise of the withdrawal power by the beneficiary, including assets which may be payable to the trust over time, such as IRAs. [Note that the "deemed release" amount will therefore vary, depending on whether or not you choose to follow the 9th Circuit's decision in *Fish*.] Because of the hanging power, even if *Fish* applied there would be no IRC Section 2041(b)(2) or 2514(e) lapse issue.

Step 3: The current income not withdrawn by the beneficiary during the calendar year is added to the principal of the trust, and the current beneficiary retains an annual power to withdraw from the principal of the trust an amount equal to the trust's previous current income in which the beneficiary's withdrawal power did not lapse at the end of any previous calendar year pursuant to Step 2. This subsequent power of withdrawal over principal will thereupon lapse at the end of each succeeding calendar year, but again only to the extent it will not constitute a release under either IRC Section 2041(b)(2) or 2514(e). The trustee is given the power to use all or any portion of the trust's assets to satisfy the exercise of the withdrawal power by the beneficiary under this Step 3, other than current trust accounting income, including assets which may be payable to the trust over time, such as IRAs. Because the trust document now clearly bestows upon the beneficiary a right to withdraw trust principal in Step 3, the basis of the 9th Circuit's decision in *Fish* no longer exists.

If the beneficiary desires to accelerate the lapsing process under this 3-step plan, but without adding to the value of the beneficiary's assets, the beneficiary need merely exercise the beneficiary's power of withdrawal to pay the income taxes attributable to the Section 678 power and/or to pay other living expenses.

Sample Form

Here is a sample form which implements these "Section 678" drafting recommendations:

Section 1. Distribution of Income and Principal During Lifetime of Beneficiary

1.1 Subject to the remaining provisions of this subsection 1.1, during the beneficiary's lifetime the beneficiary (including any legal representative acting on behalf of the beneficiary if the beneficiary is under a legal incapacity) shall have the annual noncumulative power to withdraw all or any portion of the trust accounting income on or before December 31 of the calendar year (or on the date of the beneficiary's death, if earlier); PROVIDED, HOWEVER, that (i) the foregoing power of withdrawal shall not extend to the portion of the trust accounting income which, for the calendar year, would be exempt from federal income tax, and (ii) if Section 2041(b)(2) and/or 2514(e) of the Internal Revenue Code, or any successor sections thereto, is/are in effect during the calendar year, the beneficiary's power of withdrawal under this subsection 1.1 shall lapse at the end of the calendar year (or on the date of the beneficiary's death, if earlier) to the extent the same shall not constitute a release of a general power of appointment by the beneficiary pursuant to the provisions of either or both Section 2041(b)(2) and/or 2514(e) of the Internal Revenue Code, or any successor sections thereto in effect at the time of the lapse, after factoring in all other lapsed powers of withdrawal of the beneficiary other than pursuant to the provisions of subsection 1.2, below. The portion of the trust accounting income for the calendar year subject to the beneficiary's foregoing power of withdrawal which is not withdrawn by the beneficiary (including by any legal representative acting on behalf of the beneficiary if the beneficiary is under a legal incapacity) during the calendar year and in which the beneficiary's withdrawal power has not lapsed pursuant to the foregoing provisions of this subsection 1.1 shall accumulate and continue to be subject to a power of withdrawal in the beneficiary (including any legal representative acting on behalf of the beneficiary if the beneficiary is under a legal incapacity) pursuant to the provisions of subsection 1.2, below. Any such withdrawable trust accounting income which is not withdrawn by the beneficiary (or by a legal representative acting on behalf of the beneficiary if the beneficiary is under a legal disability) by the end of any calendar year (or by the time of the beneficiary's death, if earlier) shall be added to the principal of the trust estate. [ATTORNEY DRAFTING NOTE: MAY NOT WANT TO USE BENEFICIARY INCOME WITHDRAWAL RIGHTS WHEN: (1) SECOND SPOUSE,

OR (2) HIGH NET WORTH CLIENT AND NO TAX BENEFIT FOR SUCH POWER OVER NON-GST TAX-EXEMPT TRUST.]

1.2 Subject to the remaining provisions of this subsection 1.2, during the beneficiary's lifetime the beneficiary (including any legal representative acting on behalf of the beneficiary if the beneficiary is under a legal incapacity) shall have the annual power to withdraw from the principal of the trust estate an amount equal to all or any portion of the trust accounting income for all previous years of the trust which has not previously been withdrawn by the beneficiary (either pursuant to the provisions of subsection 1.1, above, or this subsection 1.2) and over which the beneficiary's withdrawal power has not previously lapsed either pursuant to the provisions of subsection 1.1, above, or this subsection 1.2. The beneficiary's power of withdrawal under this subsection 1.2 shall lapse at the end of the calendar year (or on the date of the beneficiary's death, if earlier) to the extent the same shall not constitute a release of a general power of appointment by the beneficiary pursuant to the provisions of either or both Section 2041(b)(2) and/or 2514(e) of the Internal Revenue Code, or any successor sections thereto in effect at the time of the lapse, after factoring in all other lapsed powers of withdrawal of the beneficiary during the same calendar year pursuant to the provisions of either or both Section 2041(b)(2) and/or 2514(e) of the Internal Revenue Code, or any successor sections thereto in effect at the time of the lapse, including any lapse pursuant to the provisions of subsection 1.1, above. The portion of the beneficiary's withdrawal power under this subsection 1.2 which is not exercised by the beneficiary during the calendar year and which has not lapsed during the calendar year pursuant to the foregoing provisions of this subsection 1.2 shall continue to be withdrawable by the beneficiary (including any legal representative acting on behalf of the beneficiary if the beneficiary is under a legal incapacity) pursuant to the provisions of this subsection 1.2.

1.3 Satisfactions of any right of withdrawal of the beneficiary pursuant to the provisions of this subsection 1.1 and 1.2, above, must be made in cash, although the trustee may liquidate any asset of the trust (including but not limited to by withdrawing retirement assets [as defined in ARTICLE __, below] and other assets which are payable to the trust over time and not yet paid to the trust) in order to generate said cash; PROVIDED, HOWEVER, that the trustee may not utilize current trust accounting income to satisfy the beneficiary's right of withdrawal under subsection 1.2, above. The trustee other than a trustee having any beneficial interest in the trust (other than solely as a contingent taker under ARTICLE __, below) may, in the sole and absolute discretion of said trustee, suspend, expand and/or alter the beneficiary's withdrawal power under subsection 1.1 and/or 1.2, above, in whole or in part, by instrument in writing executed by said trustee before January 1 of the calendar year in which such withdrawal power would otherwise exist. Reasons for such suspension, expansion and/or alteration may include, but shall not be limited to, overall tax savings for the trust and its beneficiaries (including remainder beneficiaries), creditor protection for the beneficiary, and unwise or immature use of withdrawn funds by the beneficiary. In the event the beneficiary shall have the beneficiary's aforesaid power of withdrawal suspended, in whole or in part, the trustee other than a trustee having any beneficial interest in the trust (other than solely as a contingent taker under ARTICLE __, below) may also, in the sole and absolute discretion of said trustee, restore the beneficiary's withdrawal power under subsection 1.1 and/or 1.2, above, in whole or in part, at any time, by instrument in writing executed by said trustee. The trustee shall be exonerated from any liability for any decision or non-decision under this subsection.

1.4 The trustee may, in the trustee's sole discretion, distribute, use or apply so much of the income and principal of the trust estate (which is not withdrawable by the beneficiary or by the beneficiary's legal representative pursuant to the provisions of subsection 1.1 or 1.2, above) as the trustee may deem necessary to provide for the maintenance, support, health care and education of the beneficiary, in the beneficiary's accustomed manner of living. In addition, the trustee may, in the trustee's sole discretion, distribute, use or apply the income and principal of the trust estate (which is not withdrawable by the beneficiary or by the beneficiary's legal representative pursuant to the provisions of subsection 1.1 or 1.2, above) as the trustee may deem necessary for the maintenance, support, health care and education of any descendant of the beneficiary; PROVIDED, HOWEVER, that (i) the needs of the beneficiary as specified above shall be the primary concern of the trustee, and (ii) neither the income nor principal of the trust may be used to limit, relieve or otherwise discharge, in whole or in part, the legal obligation of any individual to support and maintain any other individual. In determining the amounts to be distributed, used or applied for the beneficiary's descendants, the trustee shall not be required to treat each of such persons equally but shall be governed more by the particular needs and interests of each of them. The trustee other than the beneficiary and other than a trustee designated by the beneficiary who is "related or subordinate" to the beneficiary within the meaning of current Section 672(c) of the Internal Revenue Code, or any successor section thereto (substituting "the beneficiary" for "the grantor" in said Section), may, in such trustee's sole and absolute discretion, utilize the income and principal of the trust estate (which is not withdrawable by the beneficiary or by the beneficiary's legal representative pursuant to the provisions of subsection 1.1 or 1.2, above) for the purpose of purpose of paying all or any portion of the beneficiary's income taxes, directly, or indirectly by reimbursing the beneficiary for any income taxes paid by the beneficiary, including but not limited to income tax liability accruing to the beneficiary as a result of the beneficiary's power of withdrawal under subsection 1.1 or 1.2, above; PROVIDED, HOWEVER, that the trustee shall not possess the discretionary power described in this sentence if, as a consequence of possessing said power, the beneficiary is deemed to possess the same power for federal or state estate tax, gift tax, generation-skipping transfer tax, inheritance tax or other transfer tax purposes.

1.5 The trustee shall be entitled to rely on the advice of legal counsel with respect to any matter under this Section 1; PROVIDED, HOWEVER, that if said legal counsel's opinion is subsequently determined to be invalid as applied to this subsection, either as a result of a subsequently passed federal or state law, or a subsequently promulgated regulation or published ruling, or as a result of judicial decision, the matter shall be determined based on such subsequent development and not in accordance with said legal counsel's opinion.

The following additional clauses are designed to achieve income tax basis step-up on the remaining assets of the trust at the death of the beneficiary, while also minimizing estate and generation-skipping transfer taxes:

Section 2. Additional Testamentary Power of Appointment

2.1 In addition, except as otherwise provided herein in ARTICLE __ hereof [SPECIAL PROVISIONS IF RETIREMENT ASSETS ARE PAYABLE TO THE TRUST - TO BE DISCUSSED BELOW], if the beneficiary is not survived by a surviving spouse (as that term is defined for purposes of Section 2056 of the Internal Revenue Code, or any successor section thereto, or for purposes of the law of the state or other jurisdiction in which the beneficiary was domiciled at the time of his or her death, if said state or other jurisdiction has an estate or inheritance tax in effect at the time of the beneficiary's death), then to the extent it will not result in (i) the beneficiary's estate being liable for any federal or state estate or inheritance taxes (assuming no alternate valuation date or similar elections, qualified disclaimers, or deductible administration expenses), (ii) the beneficiary's estate being liable to reimburse any government for any assistance or other benefits provided the beneficiary during the beneficiary's lifetime, (iii) the beneficiary's estate or the trust being automatically subject to income tax on any gain attributable to any portion of the remaining trust assets, or (iv) a reduction in the federal income tax basis of any asset over its historical federal income tax basis, the beneficiary shall have the power to appoint those remaining trust assets, if any, beginning with the asset or assets having the greatest amount of built-in appreciation (calculated by subtracting the trust's income tax basis from the fair market value on the date of death of the beneficiary), as a percentage of the fair market value of such asset or assets on the date of death of the beneficiary, to the creditors of the beneficiary's estate (or to or among the beneficiary's estate and any one or more individuals and/or entities, including a trust or trusts, if the power to distribute such assets to the creditors of the beneficiary's estate is not sufficient to cause a federal income tax basis adjustment under IRC Section 1014, or any successor section thereto, at the beneficiary's death), utilizing the same appointment procedure described in subsection __, above; PROVIDED, HOWEVER, that if this trust has been or will be divided into two separate trusts for federal generation-skipping transfer tax purposes, the beneficiary's foregoing additional power of appointment shall apply (i) first to the trust having an inclusion ratio, as defined in Section 2642(a) of the Internal Revenue Code, or any successor section thereto, of other than zero, but only to the extent such trust is not otherwise already includible in the beneficiary's estate for federal estate tax purposes, pursuant to the other provisions of this trust instrument, and (ii) next to the trust having an inclusion ratio, as defined in Section 2642(a) of the Internal Revenue Code, or any successor section thereto, of zero; PROVIDED FURTHER, HOWEVER, that if the beneficiary is the beneficiary of more than one trust which includes a provision similar to this sentence, under no circumstance shall the beneficiary's estate be liable for any federal or state estate or inheritance tax as a consequence of the beneficiary's foregoing additional power of appointment, and if necessary to carry out this intent, the extent of the beneficiary's foregoing additional power of appointment shall be reduced in proportion to the value of all other trust assets subject to a similar additional power of appointment, or by a greater amount, if further necessary.

2.2 If the beneficiary is survived by a surviving spouse (as that term is defined for purposes of Section 2056 of the Internal Revenue Code, or any successor section thereto, or for purposes of the law of the state or other jurisdiction in which the beneficiary was domiciled at the time of his or her death, if said state or other jurisdiction has an estate or inheritance tax in effect at the time of the beneficiary's death), the beneficiary shall only possess the beneficiary's foregoing additional power of appointment to the same or lesser extent that the trustee (other than the beneficiary and other than a trustee who is "related or subordinate" to the beneficiary within the meaning of current Section 672(c) of the Internal Revenue Code (substituting "the beneficiary" for "the grantor" in said Section)) shall direct by instrument in writing filed with the trust during the beneficiary's lifetime and not revoked by said trustee prior to the beneficiary's death; PROVIDED, HOWEVER, that the trustee shall not possess the foregoing power to direct if the beneficiary appointed the trustee who or which possesses the foregoing power to direct, and if as a consequence the beneficiary is deemed to possess the foregoing power to direct for federal or state estate tax or inheritance tax purposes. In exercising said trustee's broad discretionary power in determining whether and to what extent the beneficiary shall possess the beneficiary's foregoing power of appointment if the beneficiary is survived by a surviving spouse, said trustee shall be primarily concerned with minimizing overall income and transfer taxes to the beneficiary's estate, to the beneficiary's surviving spouse's estate, and to recipients of the trust assets after the beneficiary's death, and with minimizing the liability of the beneficiary's estate to reimburse any government for any assistance or other benefits provided the beneficiary during the beneficiary's lifetime. The trustee shall be entitled to rely on the advice of legal counsel with respect to any matter under this subsection 2.2; PROVIDED, HOWEVER, that if said legal counsel's opinion is subsequently determined to be invalid as applied to this subsection, either as a result of a subsequently passed federal or state law, or a subsequently promulgated regulation or published ruling, or as a result of judicial decision, the matter shall be determined based on such subsequent development and not in accordance with said legal counsel's opinion.

If no action is taken by an independent trustee pursuant to the immediately above subsection 2.2, it may still be possible for the beneficiary to create an optimum level of income tax basis step-up at the beneficiary's death by intentionally triggering the so-called Delaware Tax Trap. [See the discussion at pages 74-79.]

In attempting to achieve an optimum income tax basis step-up level when the beneficiary has a spouse, the independent trustee or testator must first recognize that, to the extent the independent trustee adds a general testamentary power of appointment to, or the testator triggers the Delaware Tax Trap over, an accumulation trust having a zero inclusion ratio, and as a result assets are appointed in favor of the testator's descendants and/or a bypass trust for the benefit of the testator's surviving spouse and/or descendants (i.e., rather than to the surviving spouse and/or a QTIP Trust for the benefit of the surviving spouse where the QTIP election is made), this action will reduce the availability of the portability election to the surviving spouse.

Thus, should the surviving spouse have a significant estate of his or her own, including property which was acquired from the testator and property which was jointly-owned with the testator, federal and state estate taxes may be owed by the surviving spouse's estate which would not have been owed had the portability election been preserved by not intentionally causing estate tax inclusion solely for income tax basis purposes. Appointing the trust assets to the surviving spouse and/or to a QTIP trust for the surviving spouse will create income tax basis without disturbing the availability of the portability election, but of course at the expense of increasing the size of the surviving spouse's taxable estate.

Impact of the 2019 Year-End Tax Changes

As first discussed in chapter I, commentators appear to be almost uniform in proclaiming the demise of so-called stretch IRA and other defined contributions plan benefits (including 401Ks) after the SECURE Act. Whereas prior to 2020 designated beneficiaries could defer receipt of IRA and other defined contribution plan benefits over their lifetimes, the new rules generally place a ceiling of 10 years on this deferral. Thus, for example, with certain exceptions including a surviving spouse, a designated beneficiary having a 30-year life expectancy, who previously could have deferred receipt of the IRA or plan benefits over 30 years, must now fully withdraw the benefits within 10 years of the plan participant's or IRA owner's death. Note that under the new law there is no requirement that the IRA, etc., funds be withdrawn under any set schedule during the 10 years, as long as they are all withdrawn within 10 years. [See new IRC Section 401(a)(9)(H)(i)].[4]

Also as first discussed in chapter I, the two-fold concern created by the new tax law is that not only must all of the tax on the IRA, etc., be paid much earlier than in the past, but the tax rate on the receipts will likely be much higher than in the past, due to the bunching of income during a period when the recipients are likely to be in their peak earning years, e.g., ages 55 through 65.

Planning When Beneficiaries in Different Tax Situations

As discussed in chapter IV, one planning idea is for an individual to consider paying all or part of the IRA or defined contribution plan portion of the individual's estate to lower income tax bracket beneficiaries, where possible.

---

[4]It is important to point out initially that, although at the outset of new subparagraph (H) the new rules are said to apply only "in the case of a defined contribution plan," at the conclusion of new subparagraph (H) is a provision which deems "all eligible retirement plans (as defined in section 402(c)(8)(B)," other than defined benefit plans, to be defined contribution plans for purposes of applying the provisions of subparagraph (H). This includes IRAs and 401k plans, among all other eligible retirement plans other than pension plans. See IRC Section 401(a)(9)(H)(vi).

The theory here is that, if we have to live with the new tax law, at least minimize its effects by planning our estates in a tax-wise manner.

Of course, compensating adjustments should be made for the fact that the children will be receiving differing amounts of taxable income. The amount of these compensating adjustments may need to be changed over time, depending on all relevant factors, including the children's anticipated near-term future income tax situations.

Here is a sample form to illustrate one type of "tax adjustment" clause which can be used as part of this option:

Special Adjustment Where Retirement Assets Not Distributed Consistently. If, upon the death of the grantor, via beneficiary designation, the grantor's retirement assets (as defined in ARTICLE __, below) are not distributed to or in trust for the benefit of the grantor's descendants on a per stirpes basis (the term "per stirpes" being defined in ARTICLE __, below), then, notwithstanding any other provision of this instrument to the contrary, in distributing the shares of the trust estate passing pursuant to the provisions of ARTICLE __ hereof, the value, as of the date of the grantor's death, of all retirement assets which are distributed to any individual or trust via beneficiary designation (valued as of the date of the grantor's death) shall be added to the value of all of the assets passing under ARTICLE __ hereof for the purposes of determining the shares under said ARTICLE, and the share or shares of the individuals or trusts under said ARTICLE shall then be reduced (but not below zero) by the amount (as so valued) of retirement assets passing to the individual or trust via beneficiary designation.

Second Marriage Situations

If the estate planning attorney is faced with a second marriage estate planning situation, especially one where each spouse has a child or children from a previous marriage, oftentimes the couple may choose to leave a portion of their separate estates to the new spouse, if he or she survives, and the balance to his or her own child or children. In this frequently-experienced situation, which is the most "tax-wise" asset to leave to the surviving spouse and which is the most tax-wise asset to leave to the children?

Given the fact that the post-death deferral rules have not changed for IRA and 401K proceeds left to a surviving spouse, but like amounts left to children (other than children who have not attained the age of majority) must now be distributed within 10 years after the owner's death, the previous advantage of leaving the IRA or 401K to the children, so that they may defer receipt of the same over a much longer period than the surviving spouse, may no longer be the case. It may actually make more sense today to use a portion of the IRA or 401K to fund the surviving spouse's share, in order to avoid the new requirement that accelerates the distribution of the IRA or 401K proceeds in the case of distributions to a child or children.

Additional Drafting Considerations for Payments of IRAs, etc. to Trusts

Does paying IRA, etc., funds to trusts after the death of the account owner, to protect the funds for the beneficiary, including protection against lawsuits, divorce, and estate taxes, still make sense under the new law? Many will argue it does not, because of the high income tax rates on trusts which will now apply, in full force, when IRA, etc., proceeds are paid to a trust over a maximum of 10 years.

Recall the above discussion, however, to the effect that the high income tax rates on trusts can be addressed through the judicious use of Section 678 of the Internal Revenue Code in the drafting of the trust, which causes the income of the trust to be taxed at the beneficiary's income tax rates, and not the trust's rates. Lapsing these withdrawal rights only to the extent of 5% of the trust annually will not only eliminate any potential adverse estate or gift tax consequences, but in most jurisdictions will also eliminate any potential asset protection issues on the annual lapsed withdrawal rights.

Thus far we have been discussing tax saving strategies applicable to so-called "accumulation trusts." These same strategies will not work in the case of so-called "conduit trusts," because conduit trusts mandate that all IRA and plan distributions paid to the trust in turn be paid out to the designated beneficiary of the trust, upon receipt. Conduit trusts obviously solve the high trust tax rate issues associated with the compressed 10-year deferral period, but at the expense of obviating the reasons estate planning attorneys use trusts in the first place, e.g., asset protection, estate tax protection and divorce protection, along with general protection for young and/or spendthrift children.

Despite their advantages over conduit trusts in most instances under the new tax law [see the discussion on "eligible designated beneficiaries," below, for situations where conduit trusts may be preferable], existing accumulation trusts may still need to be modified in order to ensure the 10-year deferral period for payments to a "designated beneficiary" is achieved over the 50% shorter 5-year default period. If the shorter 5-year default period is imposed, it will be almost impossible to navigate the high income tax rates on trusts, even utilizing the combination of the IRC Section 678 and other tax savings strategies discussed above. This is because the IRA, etc., payments will be 20% or more per year, under the 5-year default rule.

It is thus incumbent on the drafting attorney to ensure that the trust qualifies under the 10-year alternate period in the case of payments to a "designated beneficiary" as defined in new IRC Section 401(a)(9)(E)(i). See IRC Section 401(a)(9)(H)(I).

Even though life expectancy is irrelevant to the new 10-year rule, there remains a concern that provisions like this one found in current Section 1.401(a)(9)-4, A-1 of the Regulations, may nevertheless still apply:

"A designated beneficiary need not be specified by name in the plan or by the employee to the plan in order to be a designated beneficiary so long as the individual who is to be the beneficiary is identifiable under the plan. The members of a class of beneficiaries capable of expansion or contraction will be treated as being identifiable if it possible to identify the class member with the shortest life expectancy."

Unless and until these regulations are revised, if the trust includes a testamentary limited power of appointment to the surviving spouse of the beneficiary, or automatically continues the trust for the surviving spouse after the death of the beneficiary, with no age limit being placed on the surviving spouse, the trust may not qualify for 10-year deferral because it is impossible to identify the class member with the shortest life expectancy. If the goal is to achieve a 10-year deferral rather than the default 5-year, there should therefore be some age limit imposed on the potential surviving spouse, e.g., no more than 100 years older than the grantor of the trust.

Similarly, the trust document should be prepared to ensure that any contingent gift cannot pass to an individual more than 100 years older than the grantor of the trust and, of course, that adopted descendants of the grantor can only consist of individuals younger than the descendant doing the adopting. Finally, charities and other non-individual beneficiaries and appointees, including the beneficiary's estate or the creditors of the beneficiary's estate, will not qualify as designated beneficiaries, because they are not individuals. IRC Section 401(a)(9)(E)(I).

Compare the situation which existed prior to 2020, where not only was it necessary to determine the class member with the shortest life expectancy, but the life expectancy of this person was the determining factor in discerning the maximum IRA, etc., payout period. To qualify for the new 10-year deferral period, it is only necessary to place some limit on the age of the class members.

If a charity (i.e., with no life expectancy) is a potential remainderman under a trust, or if, for the purpose of obtaining income tax basis step-up at the death of the beneficiary, the beneficiary is given a testamentary general power of appointment to the beneficiary's estate or to the creditors of the beneficiary's estate (each of which also has no life expectancy), the attorney drafter will need to divide the trust for the beneficiary into two shares, and ensure that in the "IRA share" it is possible to identify the individual class member with the shortest life expectancy, and that it is impossible for a non-individual to take.

Set forth below is some sample language which can be employed to accomplish the above objectives, while still ensuring that estate and generation-skipping transfer taxes are minimized at the beneficiary's death. Note the blank near the end of the first paragraph. This allows the drafting attorney to insert a minimum designated dollar amount for the trust's share of IRAs and 401Ks below which the attorney has determined that lower current income taxes and the separate share approach is not necessary, with simplicity and basis step-up for the entire trust (assuming the entire IRA/401K has been paid out over 10 years) being more desirable.

Paragraph 3 includes a special priority distribution out of Share B. This is designed to accomplish the grantor's dispositive and income tax basis step-up objectives to the maximum extent possible, while still achieving the 10-year deferral for the IRA and 401K benefits made payable to the trust.

Finally, paragraph 4 of the form has been specially designed to create an estate taxable general power of appointment in Share A of a trust which has an inclusion ratio of other than zero, without destroying the ability of the trust to defer income taxation of IRAs and 401Ks over 10 years. [As discussed at page 84, in may also be possible to create an estate taxable general power of appointment which is more sensitive to potential unusual state transfer tax issues, by utilizing a "Delaware Tax Trap" triggering device.]

Separate Accounting for Retirement Assets. If (A) one or more charitable organizations is a potential beneficiary under ARTICLE __ hereof and/or if one or more charitable organizations, the estate of the primary current beneficiary of the trust (as defined in ARTICLE __ hereof, and hereinafter referred to as “the beneficiary”), the beneficiary’s creditors and/or the creditors of the beneficiary’s estate is or are a potential beneficiary or potential beneficiaries, either during the beneficiary's lifetime or upon the beneficiary's death, or is or are a potential appointee or potential appointees of the remaining trust assets at the beneficiary’s death, and (B) (i) any retirement assets (as defined in paragraph 6, below) shall become payable to any trust hereunder as a result of the grantor’s death, whether immediately or over time, and (ii) the aggregate present fair market value (as of the date of the grantor’s death, and as determined for federal estate tax purposes, if the federal estate tax is in existence at the time of the grantor’s death, otherwise as determined by the trustee, in the trustee's sole discretion) of all of said retirement assets (as so defined) payable to the trust, shall exceed $________, then (C) the trustee shall set aside and maintain as a separate share (hereinafter referred to as "Share A") from the remainder of the assets of each trust established hereunder (hereinafter referred to as "Share B"), said trust's right to receive all retirement assets (as so defined), together with the proceeds from the same, and with respect to any such separate shares created hereunder, the following rules shall apply notwithstanding any other provision of this instrument to the contrary:

1. No portion of the income or principal of Share A may be distributed to a charitable organization or to the beneficiary's estate, the beneficiary's creditors, or the creditors of the beneficiary's estate, and no testamentary power of appointment in Share A may be exercised in favor of any charitable organization or in favor of the beneficiary's estate, the beneficiary's creditors or the creditors of the beneficiary's estate.

2. For purposes of construing the provisions of the "CONTINGENT REMAINDER INTERESTS" under ARTICLE __ hereof which will potentially apply at the termination of Share A, all charitable organization takers shall be deemed to be not then in existence.

3. If, as a result of the application of paragraphs 1 and 2, immediately above, a non-individual or non-individuals which would have otherwise received a portion of Share A, either as a result of the death of the beneficiary or as a contingent taker or takers under ARTICLE ___ hereof, is or are deemed to be not then in existence, only

these non-individual(s) shall be deemed to be designated as beneficiary or beneficiaries of Share B for purposes of determining the takers upon the death of the beneficiary and/or as contingent takers of Share B under said ARTICLE ___ hereof, until such time as said non-individual(s) receive the same share(s) in Share B which it or they would have received in Share A had it or they not been deemed to be then in existence pursuant to the application of the immediately preceding paragraphs 1 and 2, after which point the provisions applicable at the death of the beneficiary and under said ARTICLE ___ hereof shall apply normally to the balance of Share B.

4. If the trust has an inclusion ratio, as defined in Section 2642(a) of the Internal Revenue Code or in any successor section thereto, of other than zero, and if, assuming the primary current beneficiary of the trust died immediately, a "taxable termination" as defined in Section 2612(a) of the Internal Revenue Code or in any successor section thereto, would occur, then the primary current beneficiary of the trust shall have the power to withdraw all of the income and principal of Share A of the trust, but only with the consent of the then acting trustee or co-trustees of the trust (other than the primary current beneficiary of the trust or any institution in which the primary current beneficiary of the trust owns any interest) who and/or which is/are not adverse to the exercise by the primary current beneficiary of the trust of the aforesaid power of withdrawal (within the meaning of Internal Revenue Code Section 2041(b)(1)(C)(ii), or any successor section thereto, and Section 20.2041-3(c)(2) of the Treasury Regulations, or any successor section(s) thereto), or if all of the then acting trustees (other than the primary current beneficiary of the

trust or any institution in which the primary current beneficiary of the trust owns any interest) are adverse to said exercise, then only with the consent of a nonadverse individual or institution (other than the primary current beneficiary of the trust or any institution in which the primary current beneficiary of the trust owns any interest) designated by the then acting trustee or co-trustees of the trust (other than the primary current beneficiary of the trust or any institution in which the primary current beneficiary of the trust owns any interest), or, if no such nonadverse individual or institution has been designated, only with the consent of the institution (or its successor) designated herein as the sole ultimate successor institutional trustee of the trust. (The previous provisions of this paragraph 4 shall not be construed as a limitation on any trust beneficiary who is already entitled to receive all of the income of the trust currently, pursuant to the terms of the trust, or who already possesses a current right to withdraw all or any portion of the trust income or principal, pursuant to the terms of the trust.)

5. If the foregoing provisions of this Section apply to the trust, said provisions shall continue to apply to any other trust which is subsequently funded utilizing assets of the original trust, in whole or in part.

6. The term "retirement assets" shall mean any asset classified as part of a qualified plan pursuant to Section 401 of the Internal Revenue Code, or any successor section thereto, as part of an annuity payable under Section 403(a) or 403(b) of the Internal Revenue Code, or any successor sections thereto, as part of an individual retirement account (including a simplified employee pension) pursuant to

Section 408 of the Internal Revenue Code, or any successor section thereto, as part of a ROTH IRA pursuant to Section 408A of the Internal Revenue Code, or any successor section thereto, as part of an inherited IRA established by the trustee pursuant to Section 402(c)(11) of the Internal Revenue Code, or any successor section thereto, as part of a retirement plan pursuant to Section 457 of the Internal Revenue Code, or any successor section thereto, or as part of any similar qualified retirement arrangement under the Internal Revenue Code.

The "Current Income Taxation" vs "Income Tax Basis Step-Up" Tradeoff

Except in the case of a trust having an inclusion ratio of other than zero, where full federal estate tax inclusion is achieved under paragraph 4 of the above form by granting the beneficiary a lifetime general power of withdrawal over the trust income and principal (subject to the consent of a nonadverse trustee in order to preserve asset protection for the trust corpus), income tax basis step-up will not be available for the "IRA portion" of the trust. This situation arises for two reasons. First, a testamentary power to appoint to the beneficiary's estate or to the creditors of the beneficiary's estate, even when limited so that it will not cause the beneficiary's estate to be liable to pay federal or state estate or inheritance taxes, would cause the loss of the 10-year deferral for IRA, etc. receipts payable to the trust. Second, granting the beneficiary the full lifetime power to withdraw the income and principal of a trust having an inclusion ratio of zero, even if limited by requiring the approval of a nonadverse trustee, would automatically cause the *entire* trust (i.e., not just the portion which will not cause estate tax) to be included in the beneficiary's taxable estate.

Unfortunately, therefore, in an effort to achieve 10-year versus the default 5-year deferral for the "IRA portion" of a trust having a zero inclusion ratio, in the long run this drafting may necessarily cost the remainder persons of the trust significant capital gain tax dollars, because *no* income tax basis step-up would be available for the "IRA portion" of the trust at the death of the life beneficiary of the trust.

An alternative approach to creating income tax basis step-up, worth considering in certain situations, is for the Share A beneficiary of the zero inclusion ratio trust to exercise a limited testamentary power of appointment over the Share A assets at the beneficiary's death in a fashion which intentionally violates IRC Section 2041(a)(3), sometimes referred to as "triggering the Delaware Tax Trap." Although an exhaustive discussion of the subject matter is beyond the scope of this handbook, it should be noted that commentators differ whether this strategy will always be successful. Whether this approach to intentionally causing full or partial federal estate tax inclusion for a zero inclusion ratio trust should be utilized over other approaches to achieving income tax basis step-up, as well as the effectiveness of this strategy generally, will depend on all the facts and circumstances, including: (a) applicable state law, (b) the manner in which the instrument creating the limited power of appointment is crafted, and (c) the manner in which the instrument exercising the power is drafted.

Section 20.2041-3(e) of the Regulations, set out here, which is intended as an interpretation of IRC Section 2041(a)(3), is significant because it can provide the drafting attorney with a valuable roadmap for intentionally triggering the Delaware Tax Trap, in whole or in part. In studying the regulation note in particular the language which the author has bolded, which language is not part of the Internal Revenue Code language itself, or part of IRC Section 2041(a)(3)'s legislative history.

(e) Successive powers.

(1) Property subject to a power of appointment created after October 21, 1942, which is not a general power, is includable in the gross estate of the holder of the power under section 2041(a)(3) if the power is exercised, and if both of the following conditions are met:

(i) If the exercise is (a) by will, or (b) by a disposition which is of such nature that if it were a transfer of property owned by the decedent, the property would be includable in the decedent's gross estate under sections 2035 through 2037; and

(ii) If the power is exercised by creating another power of appointment which, **under the terms of the instruments creating and exercising the first power** and under applicable local law, can be validly exercised so as to (a) postpone the vesting of any estate or interest in the property for a period ascertainable without regard to the date of the creation of the first power, or (b) (if the applicable rule against perpetuities is stated in terms of suspension of ownership or of the power of alienation, rather than of vesting) suspend the absolute ownership or the power of alienation of the property for a period ascertainable without regard to the date of the creation of the first power.

The Regulation infers that the greatest chance of success for intentionally triggering the Delaware Tax Trap will lie in states which have an unlimited rule against perpetuities, and where *both* (1) the trust instrument which *creates* the first power of appointment ("the first power") *and* (2) the will or trust instrument which *exercises* the first power, allow for the valid exercise of a new power ("the second power") in a manner which can postpone or suspend the vesting or ownership of any estate or interest in the property subject to the second power for a period ascertainable without regard to the date of the creation of the first power. **[This Regulation also infers to the author that, in crafting any power of appointment, especially after the general repeal of the Rule Against Perpetuities, there should be included a clear and bold warning to the donee of the power to be cognizant of IRC Section 2041(a)(3) in exercising the power, so as to not inadvertently trigger the Delaware Tax Trap, and to employ the assistance of estate planning counsel prior to exercising the power of appointment. The drafting attorney should not assume he or she will be representing the donee of the power of appointment, in other words. This same warning can then also be used to make the donee aware that he or she may choose to**

utilize IRC Section 2041(a)(3) in an effort to create income tax basis step-up at his or her death, but again only with the assistance of estate planning counsel.]

Thus, for example, if a person who creates a limited testamentary power of appointment (the "first power") in a spouse or child resides in a state which has completely repealed the common law Rule Against Perpetuities (i.e., has not replaced it with, say, a 360-year rule),without placing any duration restraints on the spouse's or child's exercise of the first power, and if the spouse or child in turn exercises the first power by creating a new power (the "second power") in, e.g., a grandchild, which second power can be validly exercised by the grandchild so as to postpone the vesting of any estate or interest in the property for a period ascertainable without regard to the date of the creation of the first power (presumably the date of death of the grandparent), the spouse's or child's exercise of the first power should cause the trust assets subject to the first power to be includible in the spouse's or child's gross estate under Section 2041, and therefore also entitled to income tax basis step-up.

Of course, any intentional triggering of the Delaware Tax Trap must be carefully formulated so as to not cause the first power holder's estate to be liable for any federal or state estate or inheritance taxes (unless, as described in the next section of this handbook, this is desirable in order to avoid a higher generation-skipping transfer tax), as well as to cause the greatest basis step-up possible. The triggering should therefore be accomplished in a two-part exercise of the testamentary limited power of appointment, part 1 being to a trust containing an additional ("second") power of appointment violative of ("triggering") IRC Section 2041(a)(3), and part 2 being to a trust which does not include an additional power of appointment which violates IRC Section 2041(a)(3).

Here is one sample form:

1. To the extent it will not result in (i) my estate being liable for any federal or state estate or inheritance taxes (assuming no alternate valuation date or similar elections, qualified disclaimers, or deductible administration expenses), (ii) my estate being liable to reimburse any government for any assistance or other benefits provided me during my lifetime, (iii) the Trust being automatically subject to income tax on any gain attributable to any portion of the remaining trust assets, or (iv) a reduction in the federal income tax basis of any asset of the Trust over its historical federal income tax basis, I hereby appoint those remaining assets of the trust under ARTICLE __ of the JOHN DOE LIVING TRUST (herein "the Trust"), if any, over which I possess a testamentary power of appointment, beginning with the asset or assets having the greatest amount of built-in appreciation (calculated by subtracting the trust's income tax basis from the fair market value on the date of my death), as a percentage of the fair market value of such asset or assets on the date of my death, to the trust under ARTICLE __ of my Revocable Trust; PROVIDED, HOWEVER, that if the Trust has been or will be divided into two separate trusts for federal generation-skipping transfer tax purposes, this appointment shall apply (i) first to the trust having an inclusion ratio, as defined in Section 2642(a) of the Internal Revenue Code, or an successor

section thereto, of other than zero, but only to the extent such trust is not otherwise already includible in my estate for federal estate tax purposes, pursuant to the other provisions of the JOHN DOE LIVING TRUST, and (ii) next to the trust having an inclusion ratio, as defined in Section 2642(a) of the Internal Revenue Code, or any successor section thereto, of zero.

2. I hereby appoint the balance of the assets of the Trust, if any, over which I possess a testamentary power of appointment, to the trust under ARTICLE __ of my Revocable Trust.

Finally, note that in some situations triggering of the Delaware Tax Trap in the manner described above, in an effort to create income tax basis step-up at the beneficiary's death, may be the only viable alternative to creating income tax basis which is available to the beneficiary. In these situations it would normally seem that there would be nothing to lose by proceeding down this planning path.

The "Current Income Taxation" vs "Transfer Taxation" Tradeoff

There may also be a "tax tradeoff" decision to be made between potentially reducing income taxes on IRA and 401K receipts, on the one hand, and the payment of additional federal and state transfer taxes at the beneficiary's death, on the other. Set forth below is some optional conditional testamentary general power of appointment language the attorney may choose to employ when drafting a trust which will otherwise be subject to federal (and, in some situation, state) generation-skipping transfer taxes at the beneficiary's death, i.e., trusts with an inclusion ratio of other than zero. The purpose of this optional language is to minimize ***overall*** federal and state estate, inheritance and generation-skipping transfer taxes payable at the beneficiary's death by utilizing a formula conditional testamentary general power of appointment which considers all such taxes as well as the domicile of the beneficiary at the time of his or her death.

In order to enable 10-year deferral rather than five-year deferral, the first clause of the form excepts from its scope Share A situations where the trust has an inclusion ratio of other than zero and also establishes a Share A/B arrangement (the "Separate Accounting for Retirement Arrangements" clause set forth at page 69, above, which includes its own taxable general power of appointment in paragraph 4).

Note also the language throughout the paragraph which creates a formula designed to minimize overall federal and state estate, inheritance and transfer taxes at the beneficiary's death, including federal and state generation-skipping transfer taxes.

Conditional Testamentary Power of Appointment. Any other provision in this instrument notwithstanding (other than the "Separate Accounting for Retirement Assets" provision of Section __ of this ARTICLE), if a separate trust hereunder has an inclusion ratio (as defined in Section 2642(a) of the Internal Revenue Code or in any successor section thereto) of other than zero, such property may also be distributed at the primary current income beneficiary of the trust's (as defined in ARTICLE __ hereof, and hereinafter in this paragraph referred to simply as "the beneficiary") death to such of the creditors of the beneficiary's estate (or to the beneficiary's estate if the power to distribute such amounts to the creditors of the beneficiary's estate is insufficient to include such property in the beneficiary's estate for federal estate tax purposes) as shall be designated by a provision in the beneficiary's last will and testament, signed after the grantor's death, making specific reference to this paragraph. Any such property with respect to which the beneficiary fails to effectively exercise this power of appointment shall be distributed as though this paragraph were not contained in this instrument; PROVIDED, HOWEVER, that unless the beneficiary specifies otherwise in a last will and testament or trust instrument, the trustee shall pay from such separate trust all estate, inheritance and other transfer taxes (including interest and penalties) imposed by reason of the beneficiary's death which would not have been imposed were it not for the inclusion of such property in the beneficiary's estate for estate, inheritance or other transfer tax purposes. Notwithstanding the preceding provisions of this paragraph to the contrary, however, this power of appointment shall not be applicable to a particular trust if, absent this power of appointment, no distribution from the trust at the beneficiary's death would be subject to a federal or state generation-skipping transfer or other transfer tax, and this power of appointment shall only be applicable (i) to the extent it maximizes a reduction of the aggregate federal and state estate, inheritance, generation-skipping transfer and other transfer tax liability otherwise applicable to the assets of the trust as a result of the beneficiary's death or (ii) in the event this power of appointment has no effect upon said aggregate tax liability, in either case assuming no alternate valuation date or similar elections, qualified disclaimers, or deductible administration expenses. For purposes of this paragraph it shall be assumed [except to the extent the trustee (other than the beneficiary and other than a trustee who is "related or subordinate" to the beneficiary of the trust within the meaning of current Section 672(c) of the Internal Revenue Code (substituting "the beneficiary" for "the grantor" in said Section)) shall direct by instrument in writing filed with the trust during the beneficiary's lifetime and not revoked by said trustee prior to the beneficiary's death] that all available federal and state qualified terminable interest property elections or similar marital deduction elections are made in the beneficiary's estate only to the extent they have the effect of minimizing all federal and state estate and inheritance taxes applicable to the beneficiary's estate at the beneficiary's death. In the event the foregoing power of appointment shall only be applicable to a portion of the property held in said separate trust, the power of appointment shall extend first to those trust asset(s) having the greatest amount of built-in appreciation (calculated by subtracting the trust's income tax basis from the fair market value on the date of death of the beneficiary), as a percentage of the fair market value of such asset or assets on the date of death of the beneficiary. In the event the foregoing power of appointment shall have no effect upon the aggregate federal and state estate, inheritance, generation-skipping transfer and other transfer tax liability applicable to the assets of the trust as a result of the beneficiary's death, trust assets which would have a lower federal income tax basis if subject to the foregoing power of appointment shall be excluded from the same.

In the case of a trust having an inclusion ratio of other than zero, the aforesaid attempt to achieve the "optimum" estate and transfer tax level at the beneficiary's death will be hampered in a state which imposes an estate tax but which imposes no or a low generation-skipping transfer tax, if Share A of the trust is structured in the above [paragraph 4 at page 71] manner, which manner necessarily creates automatic *full* Section 2041 estate tax inclusion.

Assume, for example that a beneficiary of a trust having an inclusion ratio of one resides in a state which imposes an estate tax rate of 17% but a generation-skipping transfer tax rate of only 2%. Assume also that the beneficiary has an independent taxable estate which exceeds the available federal and state estate tax exemption amounts. Does it make sense, in this scenario, to automatically include the entire Share A of the beneficiary's trust having an inclusion ratio of one included in the beneficiary's taxable estate for both federal and state estate tax purposes?

The federal estate tax will be 40%, and the net state estate tax payable will be 10.2%, after factoring in the federal estate tax deduction for the state estate taxes paid. However, had the trust property not been intentionally and fully included in the beneficiary's taxable estate, the federal generation-skipping transfer tax rate would be 40%, but the net state generation-skipping transfer tax would be only 1.2%, after factoring in the federal generation-skipping transfer tax deduction for the state generation-skipping transfer taxes paid.

If this situation is a concern in a particular drafting case involving Share A of a trust having an inclusion ratio of other than zero, consideration should be given to utilizing an alternative route (i.e., to paragraph 4 at page 71) for causing estate tax inclusion, which route might involve intentionally triggering the Delaware Tax Trap, but only to the extent the trigger achieves the same "optimum" level of estate tax inclusion - if any - which the above sample form achieves in the case of Share B of the same trust. [See the triggering the Delaware Tax Trap discussion at pages 74-79.]

Unscrambling the New "Eligible Designated Beneficiary" Rules

The new "eligible designated beneficiary" provisions of the Internal Revenue Code are unnecessarily complex, with their multiple cross-references to various sections of the Internal Revenue Code, run-on sentences, confusing (if not misleading) terminology, etc. The goal of this section of the book is to unscramble these provisions in order to make them as comprehensible as possible for the reader.

Under new IRC Section 401(a)(9)(E)(ii), the term "eligible designated beneficiary" includes any designated beneficiary who is (I) the surviving spouse of the employee, (II) a child of the employee who has not reached "majority" (a seemingly simple word which, as defined in the regulations under IRC Section 401(a)(9)(F), specifically Section 1.401(a)(9)-6, A-15, can include a child of up to 25 years of age in certain defined situations - but who for purposes of this article will be referred to simply as: "a minor child of the employee"), (III) a disabled individual, (IV) certain chronically ill individuals, and (V) anyone else who is not more than 10 years younger than the employee.

The term "eligible designated beneficiary" is relevant because new IRC Section 401(a)(9)(H)(ii) provides that IRC Section 401(a)(9)(B)(iii), which creates an exception to the now 5-year and 10-year rule limitations "if any portion of the employee's interest is payable to (or for the benefit of) a designated beneficiary," must now be read to "apply only in the case of an eligible designated beneficiary."

The other requirements of IRC Section 401(A)(9)(B)(iii) have not been changed. Thus, (A) the portion of the employee's interest must also "be distributed (in accordance with regulations) over the life of such [eligible] designated beneficiary (or over a period not extending beyond the life expectancy of such [eligible designated] beneficiary)," and (B) such distributions must "begin not later than 1 year after the date of the employee's death or such later date as the Secretary may by regulations prescribe." If (A) and (B) are met, the qualified plan or IRA will be treated as a "qualified trust" under IRC Section 401(a)(9).

Let's unpack these new rules further. It will be virtually impossible to create a trust which exclusively benefits an "eligible designated beneficiary," because the trust will have remaindermen. Does this mean that only an outright distribution to the "eligible designated beneficiary" will qualify for lifetime deferral under the new law? The answer should be no.

Under new IRC Section 401(a)(9)(H)(iii), what happens is that if "an eligible designated beneficiary dies before the portion of the employee's interest . . . is entirely distributed, . . . the remainder of such portion shall be distributed within 10 years after the death of such eligible designated beneficiary." In the case of an individual who is an "eligible designated beneficiary" by reason of being a minor child of the employee, the 10-year payout rule begins on the earlier of the death of the child or the date the child reaches majority. IRC Sections 401(a)(9)(E)(iii), 401(a)(9)(H)(iii).

So now we have it! Trusts for "eligible designated beneficiaries" do qualify for lifetime deferral. It is just that, under the new law, other lifetime and remainder beneficiaries of the "IRA portion" of trust are irrelevant because (i) presumably other lifetime beneficiaries who are not "eligible designated beneficiaries" are not permitted if lifetime deferral is desired, and (ii) remainder beneficiaries do not matter because the trust must effectively function as a conduit trust, turning over all IRA, etc., distributions to the beneficiary upon receipt.

Because most trusts will have remaindermen who are not "eligible designated beneficiaries," it is impossible to utilize an accumulation trust (other than the "Scenario II" form of special needs trust, described at pages 91-92) if lifetime IRA deferral is the goal. To be clear, the trust can have lifetime or remainder beneficiaries who are not "eligible designated beneficiaries," as long as these "non-eligible" beneficiaries cannot share in the IRA, etc., proceeds during the lifetime or minority of the eligible designated beneficiary. Upon the death of the eligible designated beneficiary, or when an eligible designated beneficiary who is a minor attains the age of majority, the balance of the IRA, etc., account must be paid out, to anyone, including to the trust, and apparently even including to a beneficiary which does not qualify as a "designated beneficiary" (e.g., charity), within 10 years. IRC Sections 401(a)(9)(H)(iii), 401(a)(9)(E)(iii).

One thought to ponder is whether we will want to utilize this "new" conduit trust approach in the case of a minor child. Does it make tax sense to "transfer" the bulk of the IRA, etc., income to the 10 of the child's working (i.e., income-producing) years, when it could have been withdrawn by the trustee over 10 of the child's non-working years, i.e., his or her years as an unemployed minor, especially considering the obvious negatives associated with distributing IRA, etc., proceeds to a minor, or even to a conservatorship or custodianship for a minor, which the minor can freely access upon attaining the applicable age of majority.

Before turning to the special rules applicable to disabled and chronically ill individuals, there is one other category of "eligible designated beneficiaries" which needs to be studied. This category applies to any other individual "who is not more than 10 years younger than the employee." IRC Section 401(a)(9)(E)(ii)(V). This individual would normally be a close friend or relative, but of course it could be anyone who fits into the category. The important point to note is that the same analysis discussed above applicable to surviving spouse eligible designated beneficiaries, should apply here. Thus, payments to a trust for the beneficiary must be in the form of a conduit trust, at least as to the "IRA portion" of the trust, and when the beneficiary passes the remaining balance of the IRA, etc., must be paid out within 10 years, to anyone, including to the trust, and apparently including to a beneficiary which does not qualify as a designated beneficiary (e.g., charity).

Unscrambling the New "Applicable Multi-Beneficiary Trust" Rules

The new "applicable multi-beneficiary trust" provisions of the Internal Revenue Code may be even more difficult to follow than the new "eligible designated beneficiary" rules - if that is possible. We will study these rules in the same manner we studied the "eligible designated beneficiary" rules, i.e., by first attempting to understand the meaning of the term "applicable multi-beneficiary trust" and then by attempting to understand the relevance of the term.

According to new IRC Section 401(a)(9)(H)(v), an "applicable multi-beneficiary trust" means a trust:

"(I) which has more than one beneficiary,

(II) all of the beneficiaries of which are treated as designated beneficiaries for purposes of determining the distribution period pursuant to this paragraph, and

(III) at least one of the beneficiaries of which is an eligible designated beneficiary described in subclause (III) or (IV) of subparagraph (E)(ii)."

The eligible designated beneficiaries described in subclause (III) and (IV) of paragraph (E)(ii) are disabled and chronically ill individuals.

The first question which naturally arises is whether a typical special needs trust, which normally only benefits one individual during the lifetime of that individual, qualifies as an "applicable multi-beneficiary trust." Because remainder beneficiaries of a trust are still beneficiaries of the trust, and the "applicable multi-beneficiary trust" definition does not limit the phrase "has more than one beneficiary" to lifetime beneficiaries, it would appear that the standard special needs trust meets requirement (I) of the definition. Furthermore, because most special needs trusts are drafted with the disabled individual as the only lifetime beneficiary, any other reading of this Code language would render the section practically moot.

Requirement (II) of the "applicable multi-beneficiary trust" definition is that all of the beneficiaries of the trust must be "treated as designated beneficiaries for purposes of determining the distribution period pursuant to this paragraph." This is not actually a trust drafting requirement, but rather a requirement for computing the applicable distribution period for the IRA, etc., payments. What is significant here is that all of the beneficiaries "of the trust," regardless of whether they have any ability to share in the IRA, etc., proceeds which are distributed to the trust, apparently must be included in figuring out the designated beneficiary with the shortest life expectancy. This is a departure from the previous rules relative to accumulation trusts. Caution should therefore be the rule, as this may require the establishment of two separate trusts (i.e., not just two separate shares of one trust) when a special needs beneficiary is involved, one where older individual beneficiaries and/or non-individual beneficiaries (e.g., charity) can benefit, and one (i.e., the "IRA share") where they cannot.

Thus, and because "by definition" requirement (III) of the definition would have been met, the typical special needs trust which we all prepare qualifies as an "applicable multi-beneficiary trust." The next question is: How is this new term relevant in new subparagraph (H) and revised subparagraph (E)?

New IRC Section 401(a)(9)(H)(iv) provides that, in the case of an "applicable multi-beneficiary trust" (which, again, is basically a trust which has at least two beneficiaries, including remaindermen, at least one of whom must be disabled or chronically ill), two different scenarios may arise. Under the first scenario ("Scenario I"), if, under the terms of the trust, the trust is to be divided upon the death of the employee into separate trusts for each beneficiary, the lifetime payout exception under IRC Section 401(a)(9)(B)(iii) for eligible designated beneficiaries is to be applied separately with respect to the portion of the employee's interest in the IRA, etc., account that is payable to any disabled or chronically ill eligible designated beneficiary.

The language "that is payable to" any disabled or chronically ill eligible designated beneficiary does not make sense when applied in the context of Scenario I. As just described, in order for Scenario I to exist, the establishment of separate trusts for each beneficiary is required. Thus, there is no "amount payable to" any disabled or chronically ill eligible designated beneficiary, under Scenario I.

One can only surmise that perhaps what Congress intended here was to write “amount payable to any trust for the benefit of” any disabled or chronically ill eligible designated beneficiary. If this is the case (and it is impossible to tell, for sure), the intent may merely mean that such a trust will qualify for the lifetime payout exception if it structured in the same “conduit trust” fashion described in the case of a trust for a surviving spouse “eligible designated beneficiary.” Once the disabled or chronically ill beneficiary dies, the balance of the IRA, etc., must then be paid out within 10 years, again presumably to any beneficiary, including the trust or a non-individual beneficiary (e.g., charity).

Distributing the balance of the IRA, etc., to beneficiaries who are not individuals should not be problematic under the above-discussed rule that “all of the beneficiaries” of an “applicable multi-beneficiary trust” must be “treated as designated beneficiaries for purposes of determining the distribution period pursuant to this paragraph,” because in the case of a conduit trust (i.e., the Scenario I trust) remaindermen of the trust are irrelevant.

Of course, most attorneys are unwilling to draft a trust for a disabled or chronically ill beneficiary in a fashion which may disqualify the beneficiary for government aid, assuming such aid is available. This is no doubt the reason why Congress chose to add a second scenario (“Scenario II”) applicable in the case of disabled or chronically ill beneficiaries, which scenario not only solves the government aid qualification issue, but also allows other beneficiaries to benefit from the trust during the disabled or chronically ill beneficiary's lifetime, as long as these other beneficiaries cannot benefit from the IRA, etc., proceeds during the disabled or chronically ill beneficiary's lifetime.

Scenario II applies if, under the terms of the trust, no individual (other than a disabled or chronically ill beneficiary) has any right to the employee's interest in the plan until the death of all disabled or chronically ill beneficiaries of the trust. If Scenario II applies, the lifetime payout exception under IRC Section 401(a)(9)(B)(iii) applies "to the distribution of the employee's interest and any beneficiary who is not such an eligible designated beneficiary shall be treated as a beneficiary of the eligible designated beneficiary upon the death of such eligible designated beneficiary." Although there can be other beneficiaries of a Scenario II trust, even if the trust is carefully drafted so that these beneficiaries have no interest in the IRA, etc., or its proceeds, at any time, the beneficiaries will apparently still count for purposes of determining the designated beneficiary with the shortest life expectancy, and therefore the distribution period applicable to the IRAs, etc.

Note that, unlike a Scenario I special needs trust, where the remaining IRA, etc., benefits must be paid out within 10 years of the disabled or chronically ill individual's death, in the Scenario II situation Congress' apparent intent is that the pre-2020 "lifetime payout" rules apply, meaning the remainder persons of the trust would then be entitled to receive the IRA balance computed in the same manner it was during the beneficiary's lifetime. In other words, in determining whether the lifetime payout exception under

IRC Section 401(a)(9)(B)(iii) of the Code applies, as well as the designated beneficiary with the shortest life expectancy (including, potentially, the disabled or chronically ill beneficiary) for purposes of determining the payout period, we revert to this language from Section 1.401(a)(9)-4, A-1 of the Regulations which is set forth at page 66. The members of a class of beneficiaries capable of expansion or contraction will be treated as being identifiable if it possible to identify the class member with the shortest life expectancy.

This reading draws support from the fact that the Code provides that an "applicable multi-beneficiary trust" means a trust "all of the beneficiaries of which are treated as designated beneficiaries for purposes of determining the distribution period pursuant to this paragraph." The Code creates a new "class of beneficiaries" in the case of the Scenario II "special needs" trust, which includes all beneficiaries (individual and non-individual) of the special needs trust, regardless of whether any of these beneficiaries has a interest in the IRA, etc., or its proceeds.

If a non-individual beneficiary of the trust exists, including as a remainderman, it is impossible to identify the class member with the shortest life expectancy (e.g., because a charity has no life expectancy), and therefore the special needs trust will be subject to the 5-year payout period.

Under this reading of the new Code provisions applicable to traditional special needs trusts, the age of all individual designated beneficiaries of the trust, including remaindermen, becomes relevant, just as it did for all accumulation trusts prior to the year 2020. The reason these pre-2020 rules are relevant in the case of a special needs trust, but not in the case of trusts for the benefit of "eligible designated beneficiaries" generally (including non-special needs trusts for a surviving spouse of the employee, a minor child of the employee, a disabled or chronically ill individual, or any other individual who is not more than 10 years younger than the employee), is that these latter types of trusts must be drafted in a "conduit" fashion in order for the trusts to qualify as eligible designated beneficiaries, and therefore effectively there are no other beneficiaries having any interest in the IRA, etc., proceeds.

Planning Point

Applying an analysis somewhat similar to what we applied in chapter IV, when dealing with an IRA or 401K owner who has one or more special needs children or other heirs, can it make sense in certain situations to allocate all or a larger portion of the account owner's balance to the special needs trust, and then utilize the same type of trust drafting adjustments described in chapter IV?

If the IRA or 401K balance is not too large, and the account owner's beneficiaries are not too old, there may be tax wisdom associated with this plan. The trust would be able to defer income tax on the IRA or 401K balance over the special needs child's entire life expectancy (or at least the account owner's oldest child's life expectancy, if he or she is a remainderperson of the trust), instead of having to withdraw the entire account over 10 years. Of course, to the extent the annual IRA or 401K distributions to the special needs trust are not expended for the special needs beneficiary's benefit, however, they will be taxed to the trust, at potentially high income tax rates. It is for this reason that the size of the IRA or 401K, as well as the ages of the account owner's heirs, are relevant.

In a situation where the IRA or 401K balance is large and/or the account owner's beneficiaries are older, it may actually be more advantageous to allocate the IRA or 401K balance *away from* the special needs trust, again making the same type of drafting adjustments described in chapter III. Situations which fall in a middle ground would likely not benefit greatly from any special IRA or 401K allocation treatment, or at least the benefit would be speculative.

Final Thought

Most states now provide different avenues which can be explored to "amend" an existing trust in order to minimize income taxes on SECURE Act or other income of the same, without forcing the annual distribution of the trust's income into the hands of the beneficiary, and thereby disrupting the underlying purposes of the trust. These options, which include state "decanting" statutes and other measures, should be examined along with local estate planning counsel where deemed potentially desirable in a particular case.

Note, however, that none of these "trust amendment" options will affect the maximum distribution period for IRA and other defined contribution plan benefits which are already payable to the trust, nor can a "trust amendment" add beneficiaries to the trust (whether current or future) who or which did not already exist.

The estate planning team should also be careful not to cause a "grandfathered" generation-skipping transfer tax-exempt trust to inadvertently lose its exempt status as a result of an impermissible modification, or to create any other adverse estate or gift tax consequences.

About the Author

James G. Blase is a 39-year experienced estate planning attorney with offices in St. Louis, Missouri. He is also an adjunct professor in the Villanova University School of Law graduate tax program, and in the St. Louis University School of Law.

Jim spent the first 17 years of his legal career with the St. Louis law firms Thompson Coburn (then Thompson Mitchell) and Armstrong Teasdale, the latter where he also served as chair of the firm's Trusts & Estates department.

Jim is a 1981 graduate of Notre Dame Law School, where he served as Managing Editor of the *Notre Dame Law Review*, and is a 1982 graduate of the New York University Law School Graduate Program in Taxation, where he served as Graduate Editor of the *Tax Law Review*. Jim also owns a Certified Public Accountant certificate from the State of Missouri.

The author of over 60 articles for various tax and estate planning professional publications, Jim is also the author of the 2017 book *Optimum Estate Planning: Explanation and Sample Forms*, the 2019 book *Keep it for Your Children: Theodore Roosevelt's 1903 Western Trip*, the 2020 book *St. Jacinta of Fatima: The Good Shepherdess*, and the 2020 book *High Ideals: Theodore Roosevelt's 1911 Western Trip.*

www.ingramcontent.com/pod-product-compliance
Lightning Source LLC
Chambersburg PA
CBHW070253220526
45465CB00004B/1602
* 9 7 9 8 6 4 2 9 0 3 4 5 2 *